INSTANT
French
Vocabulary Builder

TOM MEANS

HIPPOCRENE BOOKS, INC.
NEW YORK

ISBN: 0-7818-0982-7

Book and jacket design by Acme Klong Design, Inc.

For information, address:
Hippocrene Books, Inc.
171 Madison Avenue
New York, NY 10016

Cataloging-in-Publication data available from the Library of Congress.

CONTENTS

Acknowledgments vii

Introduction ix

    Audio Accompaniment x

    Note on Exercises x

    Note on Answer Key x

    "False Friends" xi

    Deviations in Spelling xi

Pronunciation Guide xii

Important Note on Gender xiii

Works Consulted xiv

A Note from the Author xv

A Note to the User xv

	English suffix	**French suffix**	**Page**
Chapter 1	–al*	–al	1
Chapter 2	–ance	–ance	11
Chapter 3	–ant	–ant	17
Chapter 4	–ar	–aire	23
Chapter 5	–ary	–aire	27
Chapter 6	–ble	–ble	33
Chapter 7	–ct	–ct	43
Chapter 8	–ence	–ence	47
Chapter 9	–ent	–ent	53
Chapter 10	–gy	–gie	63
Chapter 11	–ic	–ique	69
Chapter 12	–ical	–ique	81
Chapter 13	–id	–ide	87
Chapter 14	–ism	–isme	91

Chapter 15	–ist	–iste	99
Chapter 16	–ive	–if (–ive)	107
Chapter 17	–or	–eur	115
Chapter 18	–ory	–orie	123
Chapter 19	–ous	–eux (–euse)	127
Chapter 20	–sion	–sion	135
Chapter 21	–sis	–se	143
Chapter 22	–tion	–tion	147
Chapter 23	–ty	–té	169

Answer Key 181

Appendix: CD Track Listing 193

About the Author. 195

excluding words ending in "–ical," which is a separate Chapter

ACKNOWLEDGMENTS

I would like to give special thanks to Caitlin Davis, whose research helped make this book possible. Many thanks also to Marie-Cécile Vidican, whose translations of the stories and general consulting was invaluable. Thanks also to Jean-Christophe Henry and Bernadette Hoefer. Thanks to Gina Reid, Howard Means, and my parents, Tom and Anita, for incredible support. Thanks to my editor, Anne Kemper, for her steady and enthusiastic guidance, and also to my former editor, Caroline Gates.

I would like to express my gratitude to all the foreign language teachers who have clearly demonstrated many of these patterns in the past, especially Margarita Madrigal and Michel Thomas.

Finally, much love and thanks to my better half, Aimee, for her support and encouragement throughout the creation of the entire series.

INTRODUCTION

Instant French Vocabulary Builder can add thousands of words to your French vocabulary. It is designed to be a supplement for students of French at all levels. This book will help a student to learn to communicate effectively by dramatically increasing his/her French vocabulary.

There are thousands of English words that are connected to their French counterparts by word-ending patterns. This guide will illustrate those patterns and demonstrate how easily they work. The principal reason behind this is historical—the Norman Conquest. In the year 1066 the French conquered the British Isles and ruled there for many years, introducing thousands of French words into English. This means the two languages share thousands of closely related words, which makes vocabulary building much easier.

Vocabulary building is one of the keys for successful language learning. This book presents vocabulary patterns between English and French in such a systematic fashion that expanding your vocabulary will be easy and enjoyable. I believe it is the only one of its kind.

Instant French Vocabulary Builder is very easy to use. The 23 patterns presented in this book are based on word-endings (suffixes) and the chapters are listed alphabetically. For example, the first chapter presents English words that end in "–al" (capital, normal, etc.) Many of these words end in "–al" in French also (*capital, normal,* etc.)

The second chapter presents English words that end in "–ance" (distance, importance, etc.) Many of these words also end in "–ance" in French (*distance, importance,* etc.) In other cases, you only need to slightly change the ending of the English word to arrive at the correct French word. These words are commonly referred to as cognates: words related by common derivation or descent.

AUDIO ACCOMPANIMENT: This book comes with an enclosed compact disc. Every chapter contains many recorded words that typify how words under that pattern are pronounced—all words **in bold** are on the recording. After each French word there will be a pause—it is important for the reader to imitate the native speaker during that pause.

Every chapter also contains common phrases and expressions that are recorded on the audio accompaniment. After every recorded expression there will be a pause for the reader to imitate the native speaker. All expressions **in bold** are on the recording.

In the exercise section of each chapter there are stories for the student to read and listen to with questions that follow. These stories are **in bold** and are also on the recording. They are read by a native speaker at standard speed. Students are not expected to understand every word of each story, but it is important for language learners to hear new vocabulary words used in an authentic context by a native speaker.

EXERCISES: At the end of every chapter, there are exercises for the student to do. The first exercise is a matching exercise that reinforces the new words learned in the chapter. The second exercise is a story followed by questions. Every chapter contains a short story about Philippe and Marie, two young French people traveling through France.

ANSWER KEY: Answers for the exercises are available in the Answer Key section.

"FALSE FRIENDS":

Sometimes the English word and the French word will look alike and sound alike, but have different meanings. These are often referred to as "false friends" or "false cognates." When this is the case, a more appropriate definition will be provided alongside the translation. One such example can be seen with the English word "library."

ENGLISH . . . . FRENCH

tutor . . . . tuteur *(meaning "guardian")*

In some rare cases, the English and French words possess such different meanings that the pair was not included in this book. For example, the meaning of the English word "appointment" has no relation to the meaning of the French word *appointements* (salary). In other rare cases, overly technical words were not included in this book.

DEVIATIONS IN SPELLING:

Precise spelling of the French words may differ from the English words in more ways than just the endings. If you are interested in spelling the word correctly, please pay close attention to the French column. For example,

ENGLISH . . . . FRENCH

incredible . . . . incroyable

PRONUNCIATION GUIDE: *All bolded words in this brief pronunciation guide are recorded on the accompanying CD,* **Track 24**.

First, let's take a look at how French vowels are pronounced:

French vowel	Example	Approximate English sound
A	**parler**	ah
É	**téléphone**	h<u>ay</u>
È	**très**	eh
I, Y	**merci**	ee
O	**Bordeaux**	oh
U	**université**	ooh

FRENCH NASAL COMBINATIONS

The following French nasal combinations and vowel combinations do not have English equivalents. Please listen to the accompanying CD to familiarize yourself with them:

Nasal combinations		French examples
an, am, en, em	=	*France, pense*
in, im, ain, aim, ein, yn, ym	=	*vin, faim*
on, om	=	*bonbon, ombre*

French vowel combinations		French examples
ou	=	*tour, cours*
ai, ei, ay, ey	=	*faire, meilleur*
oi, oy	=	*moi, voyage*
eu	=	*heure, peur*
au, eau	=	*chaud, beau*

There are a few pairings that produce distinct sounds that we will go over next.

The following combinations with the letter "c" and "ç" always produce a soft sound, as in "<u>c</u>ity": "ce," **cerise** (cherry); "ci," **cité** (city); "ça," **façade** (facade); "ço," **glaçon** (ice cube); "çu," **déçu** (disappointed)

The "j" produces a sound similar to the "s" in the English word "plea<u>s</u>ure": **jardin** (garden)

The pairings "ge" and "gi" produce the same sound as above: **plage** (beach), **magique** (magical). The pairings "gea," "geo," and "geu" also produce the same sound: **mangeant** (eating), **plongeon** (dive), **avantageux** (advantageous)

A single "s" between two vowels sounds like the English "z" or "s" in "easy": **maison** (house), **magasin** (store)

The "ch" sounds like the "ss" in the English word "pa<u>ss</u>ion": **charme** (charm), **chemise** (shirt)

The "ill" sounds like the English word "eye": **taille** (size); **maillot** (bathing suit)

The "gn" is close to the "ny" in "ca<u>ny</u>on": **gagner** (to win); **régner** (to reign)

Lastly, the letter "h" is silent in French: **hôtel** (hotel), **cathédrale** (cathedral)

IMPORTANT NOTE ON GENDER: Unless otherwise noted in the chapter introduction, all French nouns and adjectives listed in this book are in the singular, masculine form. All nouns are listed without the article that typically accompanies them.

WORKS CONSULTED:

Dictionnaire Hachette Oxford, Français-Anglais Anglais-Français, Le dictionnaire bilingue interactif. New York: Oxford University Press; Paris: Hachette Multimedia, 1997.

Larouse French/English English/French Dictionary, Unabridged. Paris: Larousse, 1993.

Merriam-Webster's Collegiate Dictionary, Tenth Edition. Springfield, MA: Merriam-Webster, 2000.

Kirk-Greene, C. W. E. *NTC's Dictionary of Faux Amis.* Chicago: NTC Publishing Group, 1990.

Oates, Michael and Oukada, Larbi. *Entre Amis, 4th Edition.* Boston: Houghton-Mifflin Company, 2002.

Thody, Philip and Evans, Howard. *Mistakable French, Faux Amis and Key Words.* New York: Hippocrene Books, 1998.

Thomas, Michel. *French with Michel Thomas.* Chicago: NTC Publishing Group, 2000.

A NOTE FROM THE AUTHOR

When I first started studying French, I translated an old trick I had learned from Italian: Most English words that end in "–tion" stay the same in French. I was confident that my *communication* would be fine for any *situation* in which I would find myself. I was sure that everyone would have plenty of *admiration* for my mastery of French!

I know that this vocabulary bridge has aided my French skills greatly and fed my enthusiasm for learning and using a beautiful language.

In this book I have collected the 23 most common and applicable vocabulary bridges that exist between English and French. I have done this in the hope that readers find the same immediate application I did early in my language studies. I hope you find them useful.

A NOTE TO THE USER

The focus of this book is on vocabulary development. However, as with all effective language materials, the vocabulary has been set in an authentic cultural context with realistic characters and stories to encourage immediate applicability in real-life situations.

The exercises are suitable for individual and group work. Teachers will find that the 23 chapters easily can be incorporated into a one-year curriculum.

Chapter 1

Many English words ending in "–al" have the same ending in French (excluding words ending in "–ical," which is a separate chapter).

French words ending in "–al" are usually adjectives. For example,

a <u>general</u> idea = *une idée <u>générale</u>*

ENGLISH . . . . FRENCH

All words and phrases in bold are on **Track 1** *of the accompanying CD.*

abdominal . . . . abdominal
abnormal . . . . anormal
admiral . . . . amiral
adverbial . . . . adverbial
amoral . . . . amoral
ancestral . . . . ancestral
animal . . . . **animal**
   "It's an animal." . . . . **« C'est un animal. »**
anticolonial . . . . anticolonial
antisocial . . . . antisocial
arsenal . . . . arsenal
artisanal . . . . artisanal
asocial . . . . asocial
astral . . . . astral
autumnal . . . . automnal
axial . . . . axial

banal . . . . banal
baptismal . . . . baptismal
bestial . . . . bestial
bifocal . . . . bifocal

bilateral . . . . bilatéral

brutal. . . . . **brutal**

    "It's a brutal reaction." . . . . . . **« C'est une réaction brutale. »**

canal . . . . canal *(also used for "TV channel")*

capital . . . . **capital** *(used for finance or "important";*
                                for geography, use "capitale")

cardinal . . . . cardinal

carnival . . . . carnaval *(also used for period of*
                                "Mardi Gras")

causal . . . . causal

central . . . . **central**

cerebral . . . . cérébral

ceremonial . . . . cérémonial

collateral . . . . collatéral

colonial . . . . colonial

colossal . . . . colossal

commercial. . . . . commercial *(only an adjective)*

communal. . . . . communal

confessional . . . . confessionnal

conjugal. . . . . conjugal

continental . . . . **continental**

convivial. . . . . convivial

cordial . . . . cordial

corporal . . . . caporal

crucial . . . . **crucial**

    "It's a crucial element." . . . . . **« C'est un élément crucial. »**

decimal . . . . décimal

departmental. . . . . départemental

diagonal. . . . . **diagonal**

dictatorial. . . . . dictatorial

disloyal . . . . déloyal

doctoral . . . . doctoral

doctrinal. . . . . doctrinal

dorsal . . . . dorsal

ducal . . . . ducal

editorial . . . . éditorial
electoral . . . . électoral
Episcopal . . . . èpiscopal
equal . . . . **égal**
equatorial . . . . équatorial
equilateral . . . . équilatéral
experimental . . . . expérimental

facial . . . . facial
familial . . . . familial
fatal . . . . fatal *(also used for "inevitable")*
federal . . . . fédéral
fetal . . . . fœtal
feudal . . . . féodal
final . . . . **final**
fiscal . . . . fiscal
floral . . . . floral
focal . . . . focal
frontal . . . . frontal
frugal . . . . frugal
fundamental . . . . **fondamental**

gastrointestinal . . . . gastro-intestinal
general . . . . **général**
genial . . . . génial *(meaning "brilliant," "fantastic")*
genital . . . . génital
germinal . . . . germinal
glacial . . . . glacial *(meaning "freezing cold")*
global . . . . global
guttural . . . . guttural

hexagonal . . . . hexagonal
horizontal . . . . horizontal
hormonal . . . . hormonal

hospital . . . . **hôpital**

ideal . . . . **idéal**
illegal. . . . . **illégal**
   "Stealing is illegal.". . . . . . . **« Voler, c'est illégal. »**
immoral . . . . immoral
impartial. . . . . impartial
imperial . . . . impérial
inaugural . . . . inaugural
infernal . . . . infernal
infinitesimal . . . . infinitésimal
initial . . . . **initial**
instrumental . . . . instrumental *(only used in a musical*
                                              context)
integral . . . . intégral
intercontinental . . . . intercontinental
international . . . . **international**
   "It's an international airport." . . . **« C'est un aéroport international. »**
intestinal. . . . . intestinal

journal . . . . journal *(also used for "newspaper")*
jovial . . . . jovial

lateral . . . . latéral
legal . . . . **légal**
lethal . . . . létal *(more commonly "mortel" or "fatal")*
liberal . . . . libéral
literal . . . . littéral
local . . . . local *(also used for "commercial*
                                         premises")
longitudinal. . . . . longitudinal
loyal . . . . loyal

marginal. . . . . marginal
marital . . . . marital
marshal . . . . maréchal

marsupial . . . . marsupial

martial . . . . martial

matrimonial . . . . matrimonial

medical . . . . médical

medicinal . . . . médicinal

medieval . . . . médiéval

memorial . . . . mémorial *(only a noun)*

mental . . . . **mental**

meridional . . . . méridional *(meaning "Southern")*

metal . . . . métal

mineral. . . . . minéral

minimal . . . . minimal

monumental . . . . monumental

moral. . . . . moral

multinational. . . . . multinational *(also used for "international company")*

municipal . . . . municipal

mural. . . . . mural

musical. . . . . musical

nasal . . . . nasal

natal . . . . natal

national . . . . **national**

naval . . . . naval

nominal . . . . nominal

normal . . . . normal

numeral . . . . numéral

nuptial . . . . nuptial

octagonal. . . . . octogonal

occidental. . . . . occidental *(meaning "Western")*

optimal. . . . . optimal

oral . . . . oral

orbital . . . . orbital

orchestral . . . . orchestral

ordinal. . . . . ordinal

oriental . . . . oriental *(meaning "Eastern")*
original . . . . **original**
    "It's an original idea!" . . . . . . **« C'est une idée originale ! »**
ornamental . . . . ornemental

papal . . . . papal
paradoxical . . . . paradoxal
paranormal . . . . paranormal
parental . . . . parental
parochial . . . . paroissial
partial . . . . partial *(only used for "biased")*
pastoral . . . . pastoral
patriarchal . . . . patriarcal
pectoral . . . . pectoral
penal . . . . pénal
phenomenal . . . . phénoménal
pictorial . . . . pictural
postal . . . . postal
postnatal . . . . postnatal
primal . . . . primal *(more commonly "primitif")*
primordial . . . . primordial
principal . . . . **principal**
professorial . . . . professoral
proverbial . . . . proverbial
provincial . . . . provincial

racial . . . . racial
radial . . . . radial
radical . . . . radical
recital . . . . récital
rectal . . . . rectal
regional . . . . **régional**
rival . . . . rival
royal . . . . royal
rural . . . . rural

sculptural . . . . sculptural

senatorial . . . . sénatorial

sentimental . . . . sentimental

sepulchral . . . . sépulcral

signal . . . . signal

social . . . . **social** *(more commonly "sociable")*

spatial . . . . spatial

special . . . . **spécial**

    "It's a very special day." . . . . **« C'est un jour très spécial. »**

spectral . . . . spectral

spiral . . . . spiral *(more commonly "en spirale")*

structural . . . . structural

subliminal . . . . subliminal

terminal . . . . terminal

territorial . . . . territorial

testimonial . . . . testimonial *(only an adjective; as a noun, use "témoignage")*

thermal . . . . thermal *(only used for waters, springs)*

tonal . . . . tonal

total . . . . **total**

transcendental . . . . transcendantal

transcontinental . . . . transcontinental

tribal . . . . tribal

tribunal . . . . tribunal *(meaning "courthouse")*

triumphal . . . . triomphal

trivial . . . . trivial *(also used for "coarse," "vulgar")*

tropical . . . . **tropical**

    "It's a tropical island." . . . . . . **« C'est une île tropicale. »**

unequal . . . . inégal

unilateral . . . . unilatéral

urinal . . . . urinal

verbal . . . . verbal

vertebral . . . . vertébral

```
vertical . . . . . . . . . . . . . . . vertical
viral . . . . . . . . . . . . . . . . viral
virginal . . . . . . . . . . . . . . virginal
visceral . . . . . . . . . . . . . viscéral
vital . . . . . . . . . . . . . . . . vital
vocal . . . . . . . . . . . . . . . vocal
```

Sometimes English words ending in "–al" will correspond to "–el" in French. Following are fifteen (15) of the most commonly used words that follow this pattern:

```
artificial . . . . . . . . . . . . . . artificiel
confidential . . . . . . . . . . . . confidentiel
cultural . . . . . . . . . . . . . . culturel
criminal . . . . . . . . . . . . . . criminel
emotional . . . . . . . . . . . . . émotionnel
essential . . . . . . . . . . . . . essentiel
formal . . . . . . . . . . . . . . . formel
individual . . . . . . . . . . . . . individuel (adjective only)
material . . . . . . . . . . . . . . matériel
natural . . . . . . . . . . . . . . naturel
official . . . . . . . . . . . . . . officiel
personal . . . . . . . . . . . . . personnel
residential . . . . . . . . . . . . résidentiel
traditional . . . . . . . . . . . . traditionnel
virtual . . . . . . . . . . . . . . virtuel
```

INSTANT French Vocabulary Builder

1A.

Match synonyms and/or associated words.

Reliez les paires de mots synonymes ou associés.

1. animal	convivial
2. total	unique
3. social	capital
4. original	complet
5. légal	essentiel
6. crucial	permis
7. principal	zoo

1B.

Listen to and read the story. Respond to the following questions in complete sentences.

Ecoutez et lisez l'histoire. Répondez aux questions suivantes avec des phrases complètes.

(This chapter presents the first story of the travels of Philippe and Marie. Every chapter will feature a new story about these two young French people traveling through France. Please listen to and read each story carefully before answering the questions that follow.)

Philippe et Marie sont deux jeunes de Strasbourg ; ils veulent partir en voyage (take a trip). Il y a un problème : Philippe veut faire un voyage <u>international</u> et Marie veut faire un voyage <u>national</u>. Philippe dit : « Mais Marie, ton idée n'est pas <u>originale</u>. » Marie dit : « Allons Philippe, pas maintenant (not now)! » Finalement, Marie gagne ; Philippe décide que ce n'est pas <u>crucial</u> de faire un voyage <u>international</u> maintenant. Marie a quelques idées <u>générales</u> pour leur itinéraire. Philippe dit :

« **Je ne veux pas rendre visite à ton oncle à Toulouse… il est trop <u>antisocial</u> et traditionnel !** » **Marie dit : « On va voir…** (we'll see). **»**

1. D'où sont Philippe et Marie ?

2. Quel type de voyage veut faire Philippe ?

3. Quel type de voyage veut faire Marie ?

4. Que dit Philippe de l'idée de Marie ?

5. Selon Philippe (according to Philippe), comment est l'oncle de Marie ?

-ance/-ance

Many English words ending "–ance" have the same ending in French.

French words ending in "–ance" are usually feminine nouns. For example,

arrogance = *l'arrogance*

ENGLISH . . . . FRENCH

*All words and phrases in bold are on **Track 2** of the accompanying CD.*

abundance . . . . abondance

alliance . . . . alliance *(also used for "marriage" or "wedding ring")*

ambiance . . . . ambiance

ambulance . . . . **ambulance**

   "The patient is in   **« Le patient est dans**

   the ambulance." . . . . **l'ambulance. »**

arrogance. . . . . **arrogance**

assistance. . . . . assistance

assonance . . . . assonance

assurance . . . . assurance *(also used for "insurance")*

balance . . . . balance *(more commonly "équilibre")*

chance. . . . . chance

circumstance. . . . . circonstance

clairvoyance. . . . . clairvoyance

complaisance . . . . complaisance

concordance. . . . . concordance

countenance . . . . contenance

defiance. . . . . défiance *(meaning "distrust," "suspicion")*

deliverance . . . . délivrance
dissonance . . . . dissonance
distance . . . . **distance**
dominance . . . . dominance

elegance . . . . **élégance**
extravagance . . . . extravagance
exuberance . . . . exubérance

finance . . . . finance
flamboyance . . . . flamboyance
fragrance . . . . fragrance

ignorance . . . . ignorance
importance . . . . **importance**
insignificance . . . . insignifiance
intemperance . . . . intempérance
intolerance . . . . **intolérance**

lance . . . . lance

maintenance . . . . maintenance *(more commonly "entretien")*

nonchalance . . . . nonchalance
nuance . . . . nuance
nuisance . . . . nuisance *(meaning "harmful effects")*

observance . . . . observance *(only used in a religious context)*

performance . . . . performance
perseverance . . . . **persévérance**
   "Perseverance is necessary." . . . **« Il faut de la persévérance. »**
predominance . . . . prédominance
preponderance . . . . prépondérance
protuberance . . . . protubérance

reconnaissance . . . . reconnaissance

reluctance. . . . . réluctance

Renaissance . . . . Renaissance

resistance . . . . résistance

resonance. . . . . résonance

romance . . . . romance *(meaning a genre of literature and music)*

séance . . . . séance *(meaning "session" or "meeting")*

substance . . . . **substance**

surveillance. . . . . surveillance

temperance. . . . . tempérance

tolerance . . . . **tolérance**

　　"Tolerance is a great　　　　　**« La tolérance est une grande**

　　quality." . . . . **qualité. »**

variance. . . . . variance

vengeance . . . . vengeance

vigilance . . . . vigilance

2A.

Reliez les paires de mots synonymes ou associés.

1. distance   proéminence
2. ambulance   respect
3. tolérance   hôpital
4. arrogance   parfum
5. importance   détermination
6. persévérance   loin
7. fragrance   vanité

2B.

Ecoutez et lisez l'histoire. Répondez aux questions suivantes avec des phrases complètes.

Pour organiser leur voyage, Philippe et Marie parlent de (discuss) **beaucoup de choses. Philippe parle de <u>l'importance</u> de ne pas dépenser beaucoup. Il sait qu'il y a beaucoup de <u>distance</u> à parcourir** (to cover) **et qu'il faudra** (it will be necessary to have) **de la <u>persévérance</u>. Marie elle aussi comprend <u>l'importance</u> de ne pas dépenser beaucoup d'argent. Elle demande une seule chose : elle veut voir un spectacle professionnel de danse en Corse. Philippe dit : « On va voir.... »**

1. Philippe parle de l'importance de quelle chose ?

2. Est-ce qu'il y a beaucoup de distance à parcourir ?

3. Qu'est-ce qu'il faudra ?

4. Est-ce que Marie comprend l'importance de ne pas dépenser beaucoup d'argent ?

5. Comment répond Philippe à la demande (request) de Marie ?

Chapter 3

Many English words ending in "–ant" have the same ending in French.

French words ending in "–ant" can be nouns or adjectives. For example,

elegant (adj.) = *élégant*
a restaurant (n.) = *un restaurant*

ENGLISH . . . . FRENCH

All words and phrases in bold are on **Track 3** *of the accompanying CD.*

aberrant . . . . aberrant
abundant . . . . **abondant**
arrogant . . . . **arrogant**
ascendant . . . . ascendant
assailant . . . . assaillant
assistant . . . . assistant

brilliant . . . . brillant

chant . . . . chant *(meaning "melody" or "song")*
clairvoyant . . . . clairvoyant *(meaning "clear-sighted")*
colorant . . . . colorant
combatant . . . . combattant
commandant . . . . commandant
complaisant . . . . complaisant
concordant . . . . concordant
constant . . . . **constant** *(also used for "consistent")*
consultant . . . . consultant
croissant . . . . croissant
culminant . . . . culminant

defiant . . . . défiant *(meaning "suspicious")*

deodorant	**déodorant**
descendant	descendant
determinant	déterminant
deviant	déviant
discordant	discordant
disinfectant	désinfectant
dissonant	dissonant
distant	distant
dominant	dominant
dormant	dormant

elegant	**élégant**
"He's an elegant man."	**« C'est un homme élégant. »**
elephant	**éléphant**
emigrant	émigrant
entrant	entrant
errant	errant
exorbitant	exorbitant
expectorant	expectorant
extravagant	extravagant *(also used for "odd")*
exuberant	exubérant

flagrant	flagrant

gallant	galant
giant	géant

hesitant	hésitant

ignorant	**ignorant**
immigrant	**immigrant**
important	**important**
"It's an important detail."	**« C'est un détail important. »**
incessant	incessant
inconstant	inconstant
infant	enfant *(meaning "child")*

insignificant . . . . insignifiant
instant . . . . **instant**
intolerant . . . . intolérant
irritant . . . . irritant
itinerant . . . . itinérant

lieutenant . . . . lieutenant
lubricant. . . . . lubrifiant

migrant . . . . migrant
militant. . . . . militant
mutant . . . . mutant

nonchalant . . . . nonchalant

occupant . . . . **occupant**

participant . . . . **participant**
pedant. . . . . pédant
penchant . . . . penchant
piquant . . . . piquant
pliant. . . . . pliant
pleasant. . . . . plaisant
poignant. . . . . poignant
predominant . . . . prédominant
preponderant . . . . prépondérant
Protestant . . . . Protestant *(lowercase if adjective)*

radiant. . . . . radiant
recalcitrant . . . . récalcitrant
redundant. . . . . redondant
refrigerant . . . . réfrigérant
relaxant . . . . relaxant
repentant . . . . repentant
repugnant. . . . . répugnant
resistant . . . . résistant
resonant. . . . . résonant

restaurant	**restaurant**
resultant	résultant
savant	savant
servant	servante
stagnant	stagnant
stimulant	**stimulant** *(also used for "stimulating")*
suppliant	suppliant
tolerant	tolérant
triumphant	**triomphant**
vacant	vacant *(more commonly "libre")*
vibrant	vibrant
vigilant	vigilant

3A.

Reliez les paires de mots synonymes ou associés.

1. restaurant	étranger
2. important	copieux
3. élégant	animal
4. abondant	essentiel
5. arrogant	chic
6. immigrant	dîner
7. éléphant	vanité

3B.

Ecoutez et lisez l'histoire. Répondez aux questions suivantes avec des phrases complètes.

Philippe et Marie décident de visiter d'abord une ville <u>importante</u> : Paris ! Marie dit : « Mais Philippe, c'est vrai que les gens (the people) à Paris sont <u>arrogants</u> ? » Philippe répond : « Mais ne sois pas si <u>ignorante</u> ! Non, les Parisiens ne sont pas <u>arrogants</u>, leur façon de s'habiller (way of dressing) est très <u>élégante</u> et ils savent que l'histoire de Paris est très <u>importante</u>, mais... ce sont des gens très sympathiques. » Philippe a un ami, André, qui vit à Paris et a un <u>restaurant</u> qui s'appelle <u>L'éléphant</u> rouge. Dès qu'ils arrivent (as soon as they arrive) à Paris, ils vont manger au <u>restaurant</u> d'André. Il leur sert un dîner délicieux.

1. Dans quelle ville vont Philippe et Marie ?

2. Que pense Marie des gens à Paris ?

3. Que dit Philippe de la façon de s'habiller des Parisiens ?

4. Comment Philippe décrit-il l'histoire de Paris ?

5. Comment s'appelle le restaurant d'André ?

Chapter 4

English words ending in "–ar" often correspond to "–aire" in French.

French words ending in "–aire" are usually nouns or adjectives.
For example,

> grammar (n.) = *la grammaire*
> spectacular (adj.) = *spectaculaire*

ENGLISH . . . . FRENCH

*All words and phrases in bold are on **Track 4** of the accompanying CD.*

angular . . . . angulaire
antinuclear . . . . antinucléaire

binocular . . . . binoculaire
bipolar . . . . bipolaire

cardiovascular . . . . cardio-vasculaire
cellular . . . . **cellulaire** *(mostly used for "cellular phone" in Canada)*
circular . . . . **circulaire**
consular . . . . consulaire

exemplar . . . . exemplaire

glandular . . . . glandulaire
globular . . . . globulaire
grammar . . . . grammaire

insular . . . . insulaire
intramuscular . . . . intramusculaire

jugular . . . . jugulaire

linear . . . . linéaire
lunar . . . . lunaire

modular . . . . modulaire
molar . . . . molaire *(only a noun)*
molecular . . . . moléculaire
muscular . . . . musculaire *(meaning "of the muscle")*

nuclear . . . . **nucléaire**
    "It uses nuclear energy." . . . . **« Ça utilise l'énergie nucléaire. »**

peninsular . . . . péninsulaire
perpendicular . . . . perpendiculaire
polar . . . . **polaire**
popular . . . . **populaire** *(also used for "of the*
common people")

rectangular . . . . rectangulaire

secular . . . . séculaire
seminar . . . . séminaire *(also used for "seminary")*
solar . . . . solaire
spectacular . . . . **spectaculaire**
"It's a spectacular concert!" . . . **« C'est un concert spectaculaire ! »**
stellar . . . . stellaire

thermonuclear . . . . thermonucléaire
tubular . . . . tubulaire

unpopular . . . . impopulaire

vascular . . . . vasculaire
vulgar . . . . **vulgaire**

Reliez les paires de mots synonymes ou associés.

1. spectaculaire	soleil
2. polaire	indécent
3. solaire	cœur
4. circulaire	atomique
5. nucléaire	sphérique
6. vulgaire	froid
7. cardio-vasculaire	sensationnel

4B.

Ecoutez et lisez l'histoire. Répondez aux questions suivantes avec des phrases complètes.

> **Pendant qu'ils sont à Paris, Philippe et Marie font une promenade** (go for a walk) **avec André. Pendant la promenade, le téléphone portable d'André sonne** (rings) **et il commence à parler italien. Son italien est** <u>spectaculaire</u>. **Marie est surprise qu'il parle si bien. Marie lui demande : « De quoi est-ce que tu parlais ? Ton italien est** <u>spectaculaire</u> **! » André répond : « Merci, c'était mon ami qui étudie la physique** <u>nucléaire</u>— **j'adore parler italien avec lui, mais ses conversations sont plutôt** (quite) <u>circulaires</u>, **il ne parle que de la physique** <u>nucléaire</u> **! » Marie dit : « Je suis très impressionnée, "Signor André," maintenant... où est-ce que nous allons ? »**

1. Que font-ils avec André ?

2. Quel type de téléphone est-ce qu'André utilise ?

3. Comment est l'italien d'André ?

4. Qu'est-ce que l'ami d'André étudie ?

5. Comment André décrit-il les conversations de son ami ?

Chapter 5

English words ending in "–ary" generally correspond to "–aire" in French.

French words ending in "–aire" are usually nouns or adjectives. For example,

> a dictionary (n.) = *un dictionnaire*
> extraordinary (adj.) = *extraordinaire*

ENGLISH . . . . FRENCH

*All words and phrases in bold are on **Track 5** of the accompanying CD.*

adversary . . . . adversaire
alimentary . . . . alimentaire
anniversary . . . . **anniversaire** *(also used for "birthday")*
apothecary . . . . apothicaire
arbitrary . . . . arbitraire
auxiliary . . . . auxiliaire

beneficiary . . . . bénéficiaire
bestiary . . . . bestiaire
binary . . . . binaire
breviary . . . . bréviaire
budgetary . . . . budgétaire

commentary . . . . commentaire
commissary . . . . commissaire
complementary . . . . complémentaire
contrary . . . . **contraire**
corollary . . . . corollaire
coronary . . . . coronaire
culinary . . . . culinaire

depository . . . . dépositaire

dictionary . . . . **dictionnaire**

"He's using the dictionary." . . . **« Il utilise le dictionnaire. »**

dignitary . . . . dignitaire

disciplinary . . . . disciplinaire

discretionary . . . . discrétionnaire

documentary . . . . documentaire

elementary . . . . élémentaire

emissary . . . . émissaire

epistolary . . . . épistolaire

estuary . . . . estuaire

exemplary . . . . exemplaire

extraordinary . . . . **extraordinaire**

fiduciary . . . . fiduciaire

fragmentary . . . . fragmentaire

functionary . . . . fonctionnaire *(meaning "government employee")*

glossary . . . . **glossaire**

hereditary . . . . héréditaire

honorary . . . . honoraire

imaginary . . . . **imaginaire**

incendiary . . . . incendiaire

intermediary . . . . intermédiaire

involuntary . . . . involontaire

itinerary . . . . **itinéraire**

judiciary . . . . judiciaire

lapidary . . . . lapidaire

legendary . . . . légendaire

literary . . . . littéraire

mercenary . . . . mercenaire
military. . . . . militaire
missionary . . . . missionnaire
monetary . . . . monétaire
mortuary . . . . mortuaire

necessary . . . . **nécessaire**
   "It's not necessary." . . . . **« Ce n'est pas nécessaire. »**

ordinary. . . . . **ordinaire**
ovary. . . . . ovaire

parliamentary . . . . parlementaire
penitentiary . . . . pénitentiaire
preliminary. . . . . préliminaire
primary . . . . primaire
proprietary. . . . . propriétaire *(meaning "owner")*
pulmonary . . . . pulmonaire

questionary. . . . . questionnaire *(meaning "questionnaire")*

reactionary. . . . . réactionnaire *(meaning "ultraconservative")*
revolutionary . . . . **révolutionnaire**
rosary . . . . rosaire
rudimentary . . . . rudimentaire

salary . . . . **salaire**
sanctuary . . . . sanctuaire
sanitary . . . . sanitaire
secondary . . . . secondaire
secretary . . . . **secrétaire**
sedentary . . . . sédentaire
sedimentary . . . . sédimentaire
seminary . . . . séminaire *(also used for "seminar")*
solitary. . . . . **solitaire**

stationary . . . . stationnaire
summary . . . . sommaire
supplementary. . . . . supplémentaire

temporary. . . . . temporaire
tertiary . . . . tertiaire
tributary . . . . tributaire *(only used for "paying tribute")*

unitary . . . . unitaire
urinary . . . . urinaire

veterinary. . . . . vétérinaire
visionary . . . . visionnaire
vocabulary . . . . **vocabulaire**
   "I learn the vocabulary." . . . . **« J'apprends le vocabulaire. »**
voluntary . . . . volontaire *(also used for "volunteer")*

5A.

Reliez les paires de mots synonymes ou associés.

1. nécessaire
2. ordinaire
3. contraire
4. anniversaire
5. dictionnaire
6. salaire
7. secrétaire

définition
obligatoire
argent
assistant
commun
opposé
célébration

5B.

Ecoutez et lisez l'histoire. Répondez aux questions suivantes avec des phrases complètes.

Philippe et Marie ont un <u>itinéraire</u> très compliqué à Paris. Pour ne pas oublier (in order to not forget) **leurs aventures, Marie veut louer** (to rent) **un caméscope pour filmer un <u>documentaire</u>. Un jour ils vont au Louvre, un autre jour à Notre-Dame, et un autre jour ils vont à Montmartre. Philippe dit : « Ce rythme est <u>extraordinaire</u> ! » Chaque jour, Marie filme son <u>documentaire</u>, mais Philippe ne comprend pas. Il dit : « Ce n'est pas <u>nécessaire</u> de filmer chaque détail** (every detail). **» Marie répond : « Au <u>contraire</u>, c'est très important de filmer chaque détail ! »**

1. Comment est l'itinéraire de Philippe et Marie à Paris ?

2. Qu'est-ce que Marie filme avec son caméscope ?

3. Que dit Philippe du rythme ?

4. Selon Philippe, il n'est pas nécessaire de faire quoi ?

5. Que répond Marie ?

Many English words ending in "–ble" have the same ending in French.

French words ending in "–ble" are usually adjectives. For example,

a <u>horrible</u> film = *un film <u>horrible</u>*

ENGLISH . . . . FRENCH

*All words and phrases in bold are on **Track 6** of the accompanying CD.*

abominable . . . . abominable
absorbable. . . . . absorbable
acceptable . . . . **acceptable**
accessible. . . . . accessible
adaptable. . . . . adaptable
adjustable. . . . . ajustable
admirable. . . . . admirable
admissible . . . . admissible
adorable . . . . **adorable**
    "This child is adorable." . . . . **« Cet enfant est adorable. »**
affable. . . . . affable
agreeable. . . . . agréable
amiable . . . . amiable *(meaning "friendly terms")*
applicable . . . . applicable
appreciable . . . . appréciable
arable . . . . arable
audible . . . . audible

Bible . . . . Bible
biodegradable . . . . biodégradable

cable . . . . câble
calculable. . . . . calculable

capable . . . . capable
charitable. . . . . charitable
combustible . . . . combustible
comfortable . . . . confortable *(only used for objects, not people)*

communicable. . . . . communicable
comparable . . . . **comparable**
compatible . . . . compatible
comprehensible. . . . . compréhensible
condemnable . . . . condamnable
considerable. . . . . considérable
constructible . . . . constructible
contestable . . . . contestable
controllable. . . . . contrôlable
corrigible . . . . corrigible
credible . . . . **crédible**
cultivable . . . . cultivable
curable. . . . . curable

deductible . . . . déductible *(more commonly "franchise" as a noun)*

defendable . . . . défendable
delectable. . . . . délectable
demonstrable . . . . démontrable
deplorable . . . . déplorable
desirable . . . . désirable
destructible . . . . destructible
detachable . . . . détachable
detectable. . . . . détectable
determinable. . . . . déterminable
detestable. . . . . détestable
digestible . . . . digestible *(more commonly "digeste")*
dirigible . . . . dirigeable
disagreeable. . . . . désagréable
discernable. . . . . discernable
disposable . . . . disponible *(meaning "available")*

divible . . . . **divisible**

double . . . . double

durable . . . . durable

eligible. . . . . éligible

employable. . . . . employable

ensemble . . . . ensemble

enviable. . . . . enviable

equitable . . . . équitable

estimable . . . . estimable

evitable . . . . évitable

excitable . . . . excitable

excusable . . . . **excusable**

   "The mistake is excusable." . . **« L'erreur est excusable. »**

explicable. . . . . explicable

exploitable . . . . exploitable

exportable . . . . exportable

extensible. . . . . extensible

fable . . . . fable

fallible . . . . faillible

favorable . . . . favorable

feasible . . . . faisable

feeble . . . . faible

flexible. . . . . **flexible**

formidable . . . . formidable *(meaning "great!" or "super!")*

governable. . . . . gouvernable

habitable . . . . habitable

honorable. . . . . honorable

horrible . . . . **horrible**

   "It's a horrible accident." . . . . **« C'est un accident horrible. »**

humble. . . . . humble

identifiable . . . . identifiable
ignoble . . . . ignoble
imaginable . . . . imaginable
imitable . . . . imitable
impassible . . . . impassible
impeccable . . . . **impeccable**
impenetrable. . . . . impénétrable
imperceptible . . . . imperceptible
impermeable. . . . . imperméable *(also used for "raincoat")*
imperturbable . . . . imperturbable
implacable . . . . implacable
impossible . . . . **impossible**
"That's impossible!" . . . . **« C'est impossible ! »**
impressionable . . . . impressionnable
improbable. . . . . **improbable**
inaccessible . . . . inaccessible
inadmissible . . . . inadmissible
inalienable . . . . inaliénable
inalterable . . . . inaltérable
inapplicable . . . . inapplicable
inappreciable . . . . inappréciable *(meaning "priceless")*
inaudible . . . . inaudible
incalculable . . . . incalculable
incapable . . . . incapable
incompatible. . . . . incompatible
incomprehensible . . . . incompréhensible
inconsolable . . . . inconsolable
incontestable. . . . . incontestable
incorrigible. . . . . incorrigible
incredible . . . . **incroyable**
incurable . . . . incurable
indefensible . . . . indéfendable
indefinable . . . . indéfinissable
indelible. . . . . indélébile
indescribable . . . . indescriptible
indestructible. . . . . indestructible

INSTANT French Vocabulary Builder

indispensable	indispensable
indivisible	indivisible
indubitable	indubitable
ineffable	ineffable
inestimable	inestimable
inevitable	**inévitable**
inexcusable	inexcusable
inexorable	inexorable
inexplicable	inexplicable
infallible	infaillible
inflammable	inflammable
inflexible	**inflexible**
inhabitable	habitable
inimitable	inimitable
innumerable	innombrable
inoperable	inopérable
insatiable	insatiable
insensible	insensible *(meaning "insensitive")*
inseparable	inséparable
insoluble	insoluble
intangible	intangible
intelligible	intelligible
interminable	interminable
intolerable	intolérable
invariable	invariable
invincible	invincible
inviolable	inviolable
invisible	**invisible**
invulnerable	invulnérable
irascible	irascible
irreconcilable	irréconciliable
irreducible	irréductible
irrefutable	irréfutable
irreparable	irréparable
irrepressible	irrépressible
irresistible	irrésistible

irresponsible . . . . **irresponsable**
irreversible . . . . irréversible
irrevocable . . . . irrévocable
irrigable . . . . irrigable
irritable . . . . irritable

justifiable . . . . justifiable

lamentable . . . . lamentable *(also used for "pitiful,"*
"pathetic")
legible . . . . lisible
limitable . . . . limitable

malleable . . . . malléable
maneuverable . . . . manœuvrable
measurable . . . . mesurable
memorable . . . . mémorable
miserable . . . . **misérable**
modifiable . . . . modifiable

navigable . . . . navigable
negligible . . . . négligeable
negotiable . . . . négociable
noble . . . . **noble**
notable . . . . notable

observable . . . . observable
operable . . . . opérable
opposable . . . . opposable
ostensible . . . . ostensible

palpable . . . . palpable
pardonable . . . . pardonnable
passable . . . . **passable**
payable . . . . payable
penetrable . . . . pénétrable

perceptible . . . . perceptible
permeable . . . . perméable
pitiable. . . . . pitoyable
plausible . . . . plausible
pliable . . . . pliable
portable . . . . portable *(also used for "wearable"*
                                              and "cell phone")
possible . . . . **possible**
preferable. . . . . préférable
presentable. . . . . présentable
probable . . . . **probable**
profitable . . . . rentable
programmable . . . . programmable
provable. . . . . prouvable
punishable . . . . punissable

quantifiable . . . . quantifiable

realizable. . . . . réalisable
reasonable . . . . raisonnable
recognizable. . . . . reconnaissable
recommendable . . . . recommandable
recyclable. . . . . recyclable
reducible . . . . réductible
refutable. . . . . réfutable
remarkable. . . . . remarquable
renewable . . . . renouvelable
repairable . . . . **réparable**
reprehensible . . . . répréhensible
respectable. . . . . **respectable**
responsible. . . . . **responsable**
retractable . . . . rétractable
reusable. . . . . réutilisable
reversible . . . . réversible
revisable . . . . révisable
revocable. . . . . révocable

sensible . . . . sensible *(meaning "sensitive")*
separable . . . . séparable
sociable . . . . sociable
stable . . . . **stable** *(only an adjective;*
                                   "horse stable" is "écurie")

supportable . . . . supportable
susceptible . . . . susceptible

table . . . . table
tangible . . . . tangible
terrible . . . . terrible *(also used for "great")*
tolerable . . . . tolérable
transferable . . . . transférable
transformable . . . . transformable
transportable . . . . transportable
traversable . . . . traversable
trouble . . . . trouble *(meaning "troublesome")*

unalterable . . . . inaltérable
uncontrollable . . . . incontrôlable
undesirable . . . . indésirable
unimaginable . . . . inimaginable
uninhabitable . . . . inhabitable
unrealizable . . . . irréalisable
unstable . . . . instable
untouchable . . . . intouchable
utilizable . . . . utilisable

variable . . . . **variable**
venerable . . . . vénérable
verifiable . . . . vérifiable
veritable . . . . véritable
viable . . . . viable
visible . . . . **visible**
vulnerable . . . . vulnérable

INSTANT French Vocabulary Builder

6A.

Reliez les paires de mots synonymes ou associés.

1. visible	extraordinaire
2. incroyable	rigide
3. horrible	mignon
4. inflexible	très mal
5. comparable	perceptible
6. probable	similaire
7. adorable	possible

Ecoutez et lisez l'histoire. Répondez aux questions suivantes avec des phrases complètes.

> **Après quelques jours à Paris, Philippe et Marie prennent l'avion pour la Corse. Pendant le voyage en avion ils se disputent** (have an argument). **Marie dit à Philippe : « Tu es très <u>irresponsable</u> ! Tu n'as pas reservé les places pour la danse ! » Philippe répond : « Tu es <u>inflexible</u>, nous pouvons y aller une autre fois** (another time) **; il est très <u>probable</u> que nous revenions en Corse un jour. » Marie dit : « Tu es <u>impossible</u> ! Il est assez <u>improbable</u> que nous retournions en Corse ! » Finalement, Philippe s'excuse** (apologizes) **et dit qu'il sera beaucoup plus <u>responsable</u> pendant le reste du voyage. Marie demande s'il sera <u>possible</u> d'acheter les billets pour le spectacle de danse en Corse. Philippe répond : « On va voir…. »**

1. Où est-ce qu'il vont après Paris ?

2. Que pense Marie de Philippe ?

3. Que dit Philippe de Marie ?

4. Est-ce que Marie pense qu'il est probable qu'ils retournent en Corse un jour ?

5. Que demande Marie à la fin ?

Chapter 7

Many English words ending in "–ct" have the same ending in French.

French words ending in "–ct" can be adjectives or nouns. For example,

> direct (adj.) = *direct*
> a contact (n.) = *un contact*

ENGLISH . . . . FRENCH

*All words and phrases in bold are on **Track 7** of the accompanying CD.*

aspect . . . . **aspect**

circumspect. . . . . circonspect
compact . . . . compact
contact . . . . **contact**
   "I have a good contact." . . . . **« J'ai un bon contact. »**
correct . . . . **correct**

direct . . . . **direct**
   "The train is direct." . . . . **« Le train est direct. »**
distinct . . . . distinct
district . . . . district

exact . . . . exact

impact . . . . impact
incorrect . . . . **incorrect**
   "That's incorrect." . . . . **« C'est incorrect. »**
indirect . . . . **indirect**
indistinct. . . . . indistinct
inexact . . . . inexact

instinct . . . . instinct
intact . . . . intact
intellect. . . . . intellect

respect . . . . **respect**

select . . . . sélect *(only an adjective)*
strict. . . . . strict
suspect. . . . . suspect

tact . . . . tact
tract. . . . . tract

verdict . . . . verdict

7A.

Reliez les paires de mots synonymes ou associés.

1. respect	précis
2. direct	adresse
3. correct	erroné
4. contact	immédiat
5. aspect	partie
6. exact	admiration
7. incorrect	exact

7B.

Ecoutez et lisez l'histoire. Répondez aux questions suivantes avec des phrases complètes.

Après le vol <u>direct</u> de Paris à Ajaccio, en Corse, Marie demande si leur destination est <u>correcte</u> parce qu'elle ne comprend pas tout (doesn't understand everything)**. Elle sait que le français parlé** (spoken French) **n'est pas toujours clair, mais elle ne comprend pas très bien ce <u>dialecte</u> ! Philippe dit : « Ne t'inquiète pas, j'ai un bon <u>contact</u> ici à Ajaccio, il s'appelle Alphonse, son français est excellent. » Après quelques minutes dans l'aéroport, Alphonse vient les chercher** (pick them up)**. Alphonse est très sympa et a beaucoup de <u>respect</u> pour son ami Philippe et sa petite amie Marie. Après un bon dîner chez Alphonse, Marie lui demande s'il sait quelque chose au sujet du spectacle dans le centre. Alphonse répond : « On va voir.... »**

1. Quel type de vol est-ce qu'ils ont pris (did they take) de Paris ?

2. Pourquoi est-ce que Marie pense que ce n'est pas la destination correcte ?

3. Pourquoi est-ce que Marie ne comprend pas le français en Corse ?

4. Comment s'appelle le contact de Philippe à Ajaccio ?

5. Que pense Alphonse de Philippe et de sa petite amie Marie ?

-ence/-ence

Many English words ending in "–ence" have the same ending in French.

French words ending in "–ence" are usually feminine nouns. For example,

a coincidence = *une coïncidence*

ENGLISH . . . . FRENCH

*All words and phrases in bold are on **Track 8** of the accompanying CD.*

absence . . . . **absence**
abstinence . . . . abstinence
adherence . . . . adhérence
adolescence . . . . adolescence
ambivalence . . . . ambivalence
audience . . . . audience *(more commonly "public")*

cadence . . . . cadence
coexistence . . . . coexistence
coherence . . . . cohérence
coincidence . . . . **coïncidence**
 "It's a coincidence." . . . . **« C'est une coïncidence. »**
competence . . . . compétence
concurrence . . . . concurrence *(meaning "competition")*
conference . . . . **conférence**
confidence . . . . confidence *(meaning "secret/private information")*
conscience . . . . conscience
consequence . . . . **conséquence**
convalescence . . . . convalescence
convergence . . . . convergence

decadence . . . . décadence
deference . . . . déférence
difference . . . . **différence**
divergence . . . . divergence

effervescence . . . . effervescence
eloquence . . . . éloquence
emergence . . . . émergence
eminence . . . . éminence
equivalence . . . . équivalence
essence . . . . essence
evidence . . . . évidence *(meaning "obvious")*
excellence . . . . excellence
existence . . . . existence
experience . . . . **expérience** *(also used for "experiment")*
   "He has no experience." . . . . **« Il n'a pas d'expérience. »**

flatulence . . . . flatulence

imminence . . . . imminence
impatience . . . . **impatience**
impertinence . . . . impertinence
impotence . . . . impotence
impudence . . . . impudence
imprudence . . . . imprudence
incandescence . . . . incandescence
incidence . . . . incidence *(also used for "impact")*
incoherence . . . . incohérence
incompetence . . . . incompétence
inconsequence . . . . inconséquence
incontinence . . . . incontinence
indifference . . . . **indifférence**
indolence . . . . indolence
indulgence . . . . indulgence
inexperience . . . . inexpérience
influence . . . . **influence**

innocence . . . . **innocence**

insolence . . . . insolence

intelligence . . . . **intelligence**

interference. . . . . interférence

irreverence . . . . irrévérence

jurisprudence . . . . jurisprudence

luminescence . . . . luminescence

magnificence . . . . magnificence

munificence . . . . munificence

negligence . . . . négligence

occurrence . . . . occurrence *(meaning "circumstances")*

omnipotence. . . . . omnipotence

omnipresence . . . . omniprésence

opulence . . . . opulence

patience . . . . **patience**

penitence . . . . pénitence

permanence . . . . permanence

pertinence . . . . pertinence

pestilence. . . . . pestilence

preeminence. . . . . prééminence

preference . . . . **préférence**

prescience . . . . prescience

presence. . . . . **présence**

prevalence . . . . prévalence

providence . . . . providence

prudence . . . . prudence

quintessence . . . . quintessence

recurrence . . . . récurrence

reference . . . . référence
reminiscence . . . . réminiscence
residence . . . . **résidence**
reticence . . . . réticence
reverence . . . . révérence

science . . . . **science**
   "I love science." . . . . **« J'aime la science. »**
sentence . . . . sentence *(meaning "prison sentence")*
sequence . . . . **séquence**
silence . . . . silence

transparence . . . . transparence
truculence . . . . truculence
turbulence . . . . turbulence

vehemence . . . . véhémence
videoconference . . . . vidéoconférence
violence . . . . **violence**
virulence . . . . virulence

8A.

Reliez les paires de mots synonymes ou associés.

1. patience	naïveté
2. différence	calme
3. innocence	distinction
4. violence	maturité
5. science	réunion
6. conférence	biologie
7. expérience	guerre

8B.

Ecoutez et lisez l'histoire. Répondez aux questions suivantes avec des phrases complètes.

Le jour suivant, Alphonse dit à Marie : « Quelle <u>coïncidence</u> ! Ma petite amie et moi, nous allons à la danse demain soir, vous voulez venir avec nous ? » Le lendemain (the next day)**, Marie est très contente et dit à Philippe : « Tu vois ? La persistance et la <u>patience</u> aident. » Philippe est très content que Marie soit heureuse** (that she's happy) **et pense que ça sera une bonne <u>expérience</u>. Malheureusement Philippe n'a pas beaucoup de <u>patience</u> ni d'intérêt pour la danse. Il essaie de cacher** (he tries to hide) **son <u>indifférence</u>. Philippe dit à Marie : « Je suis désolé pour mon <u>impatience</u>, mais… la danse est horrible ! » Après deux jours avec Alphonse à Ajaccio, Philippe et Marie vont à Monaco.**

1. Que dit Alphonse de la danse ?

2. Selon Marie, quelles choses aident ?

3. A quoi s'attend Philippe (what does he expect) avant la danse ?

4. Est-ce que Philippe ressent (feels) de la passion ou de l'indifférence pour la danse ?

5. Pourquoi Philippe s'excuse-t-il ?

-ent/-ent

English words ending in "–ent" often have the same ending in French.

French words ending in "–ent" can be adjectives or nouns. For example,

> different (adj.) = *différent*
> an ingredient (n.) = *un ingrédient*

ENGLISH . . . . FRENCH

*All words and phrases in bold are on **Track 9** of the accompanying CD.*

abasement . . . . abaissement
absent . . . . absent
accent . . . . accent
accident . . . . accident
accompaniment . . . . accompagnement
adherent . . . . adhérent
adjacent . . . . adjacent
adjournment . . . . ajournement
adjustment . . . . reajustement
adolescent . . . . adolescent
adornment . . . . ornement
advancement . . . . avancement
advertisement . . . . avertissement *(meaning "warning")*
agent . . . . **agent**
agreement . . . . agrément
alignment . . . . alignement
ambivalent . . . . ambivalent
amendment . . . . amendement
amusement . . . . amusement
antecedent . . . . antécédent
apartment . . . . appartement
apparent . . . . apparent

appeasement	apaisement
ardent	ardent
argument	argument *(meaning "deciding factor/point")*
armament	armement
arrangement	arrangement
assortment	assortiment
astonishment	étonnement
astringent	astringent
attachment	attachement *(only used for feelings)*
banishment	bannissement
basement	soubassement
bombardment	bombardement
cement	ciment
chastisement	châtiment
client	**client**
coefficient	coefficient
coherent	cohérent
coincident	coïncident
commandment	commandement
commencement	commencement
compartment	compartiment
competent	**compétent**
"The teacher is competent."	**« Le professeur est compétent. »**
complement	complément
compliment	compliment
comportment	comportement
condiment	condiment
confident	confident *(meaning "confidant")*
consent	consentement
consequent	conséquent
content	content
contentment	contentement
continent	**continent**

contingent . . . . contingent
convalescent . . . . convalescent
convent . . . . couvent
convergent . . . . convergent
corpulent . . . . corpulent
counterargument . . . . contre-argument

decadent . . . . décadent
decent . . . . décent
deficient . . . . déficient
department . . . . département
deployment . . . . déploiement
derailment . . . . déraillement
derangement . . . . dérangement
detachment . . . . détachement
detergent . . . . détergent
detriment . . . . détriment
development . . . . développement
different . . . . **différent**
disagreement . . . . désagrément *(meaning "annoyance")*
discernment . . . . discernement
discontent . . . . mécontentement
discouragement . . . . découragement
dismemberment . . . . démembrement
displacement . . . . déplacement
dissident . . . . dissident
divergent . . . . divergent
document . . . . document

effervescent . . . . effervescent
element . . . . élément
eloquent . . . . éloquent
embarkment . . . . embarquement
emergent . . . . émergent
eminent . . . . éminent
enchantment . . . . enchantement

encouragement . . . . encouragement

endorsement . . . . endossement

engagement . . . . engagement *(only used for "arrange-*
ment"; for marriage,
use "fiançailles")

enlargement . . . . élargissement

enlightenment . . . . éclaircissement

enrichment . . . . enrichissement

enrollment. . . . . enrôlement

environment . . . . environnement

equipment . . . . équipement

equivalent. . . . . équivalent

establishment . . . . établissement

evanescent . . . . évanescent

event . . . . événement

evident. . . . . évident

excellent. . . . . excellent

excrement. . . . . excrément

expedient . . . . expédient

ferment. . . . . ferment *(only a noun)*

fervent . . . . fervent

filament . . . . filament

firmament. . . . . firmament

fluorescent . . . . fluorescent

fragment. . . . . fragment

frequent . . . . **fréquent**

government. . . . . gouvernement

grandparent(s) . . . . grands-parents *(only used in the plural)*

harassment . . . . harcèlement

imminent . . . . imminent

impatient . . . . **impatient**

impertinent . . . . impertinent

INSTANT French Vocabulary Builder

impotent . . . . impotent

impoverishment . . . . appauvrissement

imprisonment . . . . emprisonnement

imprudent . . . . imprudent

impudent . . . . impudent

incandescent . . . . incandescent

incident . . . . incident

inclement . . . . inclément

incoherent . . . . incohérent

incompetent . . . . incompétent

inconsequent . . . . inconséquent

incontinent . . . . incontinent

inconvenient . . . . inconvénient *(only used as a noun,*
"inconvenience")

indecent . . . . indécent

indifferent . . . . **indifférent**

    "He's indifferent." . . . . **« Il est indifférent. »**

indigent . . . . indigent

indolent . . . . indolent

indulgent . . . . indulgent

ingredient . . . . **ingrédient**

inherent . . . . inhérent

innocent . . . . **innocent**

insolent . . . . insolent

instrument . . . . instrument

intelligent . . . . **intelligent**

intermittent . . . . intermittent

internment . . . . internement

investment . . . . investissement

irreverent . . . . irrévérent *(more commonly*
"irrespectueux")

judgment . . . . jugement

latent . . . . latent

ligament . . . . ligament

moment . . . . moment
monument. . . . . monument
movement. . . . . mouvement
munificent. . . . . munificent

negligent . . . . négligent

omnipotent . . . . omnipotent
omnipresent . . . . omniprésent
omniscient . . . . omniscient
opulent. . . . . opulent
orient. . . . . orient
ornament . . . . ornement

parent . . . . parent *(also used for "relative")*
parliament . . . . parlement
patient . . . . **patient**
    "You're not very patient.". . . . **« Tu n'es pas très patient. »**
pavement . . . . pavement *(more commonly "trottoir")*
payment. . . . . paiement
penitent . . . . pénitent
percent. . . . . pour cent
permanent . . . . **permanent**
pertinent. . . . . pertinent
phosphorescent. . . . . phosphorescent
pigment . . . . pigment
placement. . . . . placement
precedent. . . . . précédent
preeminent . . . . prééminent
prescient. . . . . prescient
present. . . . . **présent**
president . . . . **président**
    "Here's the new president.". . . . **« Voici le nouveau président. »**
prominent. . . . . proéminent *(only used for physical features)*
prudent . . . . prudent

quotient . . . . quotient

realignment. . . . . réalignement

recent. . . . . récent

recipient. . . . . récipient *(meaning "container")*

recruitment . . . . recrutement

re-establishment. . . . . rétablissement

refinement . . . . raffinement

refreshment. . . . . rafraîchissement

regiment. . . . . régiment

reimbursement. . . . . remboursement

reinforcement . . . . renforcement

reinvestment . . . . réinvestissement

replacement . . . . remplacement

resentment . . . . ressentiment

resident . . . . **résident**

reticent. . . . . réticent

sacrament. . . . . sacrement

sediment. . . . . sédiment

segment . . . . segment

sentiment . . . . sentiment

serpent. . . . . serpent

strident. . . . . strident

subcontinent . . . . sous-continent

succulent . . . . succulent

sufficient. . . . . suffisamment *(meaning "sufficiently," "enough")*

supplement. . . . . supplément

talent . . . . talent

tangent . . . . **tangent**

temperament. . . . . tempérament

testament . . . . testament

torment. . . . . tourment

torrent . . . . torrent

transparent . . . . transparent

treatment . . . . traitement *(also used for "salary")*

trident . . . . trident

truculent . . . . truculent

turbulent . . . . turbulent

urgent . . . . **urgent**

   "It's an urgent letter." . . . . **« C'est une lettre urgente. »**

vehement . . . . véhément

vice president . . . . vice-président

violent . . . . violent

virulent . . . . virulent

9A.

Reliez les paires de mots synonymes ou associés.

1. président	calme
2. urgent	intellectuel
3. continent	distinct
4. client	directeur
5. patient	consommateur
6. intelligent	pressant
7. différent	Europe

9B.

Ecoutez et lisez l'histoire. Répondez aux questions suivantes avec des phrases complètes.

Quand ils arrivent à Monaco, Marie appelle sa mère (calls her mother) **et reçoit un message <u>urgent</u> : elle doit rendre visite à son cousin à Monaco. Son cousin Nicolas est directeur d'un établissement médical. Philippe demande : « Décris ton cousin, comment est-il ? » Marie répond : « Eh bien, mon cousin est… <u>différent</u>… c'est un docteur très <u>compétent</u> et très, très <u>intelligent</u>, mais il est un peu étrange** (strange). **» Philippe veut savoir pourquoi il est si « <u>différent</u>. » Marie lui dit : « Tu verras** (you'll see)**, il pense que nous sommes tous docteurs."
Philippe dit : « Bon, on va voir…. »**

1. Quel type de message reçoit Marie ?

2. Nicolas est directeur de quoi ?

3. Que dit Marie de son cousin ?

4. Selon Marie, est-ce que Nicolas est intelligent ?

5. Que dit Philippe à la fin ?

Chapter 10

English words ending in "–gy" generally correspond to "–gie" in French.

French words ending in "–gie" are usually feminine nouns. For example,

a strategy = *une stratégie*

ENGLISH . . . . FRENCH

All words and phrases in bold are on **Track 10** *of the accompanying CD.*

allergy . . . . **allergie**
    "I have a lot of allergies." . . . **« J'ai beaucoup d'allergies. »**
analogy . . . . analogie
anesthesiology . . . . anesthésiologie
anthology . . . . anthologie
anthropology . . . . anthropologie
archaeology . . . . archéologie
astrology . . . . astrologie

biology . . . . **biologie**
biotechnology . . . . biotechnologie

cardiology . . . . cardiologie
chronology . . . . **chronologie**
climatology . . . . climatologie
cosmology . . . . cosmologie
criminology . . . . criminologie

dermatology . . . . dermatologie

ecology . . . . écologie
effigy . . . . effigie

elegy	élégie
endocrinology	endocrinologie
energy	**énergie**
ethnology	ethnologie
etymology	étymologie
gastroenterology	gastro-entérologie
genealogy	généalogie
geology	**géologie**
ideology	**idéologie**
lethargy	léthargie
liturgy	liturgie
metallurgy	métallurgie
meteorology	**météorologie**
methodology	méthodologie
microbiology	microbiologie
mineralogy	minéralogie
morphology	morphologie
musicology	musicologie
mythology	**mythologie**

"I'm interested in mythology." . . . « **Je m'intéresse à la mythologie.** »

neurology	neurologie
oncology	oncologie
ontology	ontologie
orgy	orgie
paleontology	paléontologie
pathology	pathologie
pedagogy	pédagogie
philology	philologie
phonology	phonologie

phraseology . . . . phraséologie
physiology . . . . physiologie
psychology . . . . **psychologie**

radiology . . . . **radiologie**
rheumatology . . . . rhumatologie

seismology . . . . sismologie
sexology. . . . . sexologie
sociology . . . . sociologie
strategy . . . . **stratégie**
  "It's an interesting strategy." . . **« C'est une stratégie intéressante. »**
synergy . . . . synergie

technology . . . . **technologie**
terminology. . . . . terminologie
theology. . . . . théologie
toxicology. . . . . toxicologie
trilogy . . . . **trilogie**
typology. . . . . typologie

urology . . . . urologie

zoology . . . . zoologie

10A.

Reliez les paires de mots synonymes ou associés.

1. allergie	temps
2. stratégie	pierre
3. psychologie	trois
4. géologie	dynamisme
5. énergie	tactique
6. chronologie	pollen
7. trilogie	mental

10B.

Ecoutez et lisez l'histoire. Répondez aux questions suivantes avec des phrases complètes.

A neuf heures du matin Philippe et Marie vont chez Nicolas. Il vit à Monte-Carlo et c'est un homme très sympathique qui a beaucoup d'__énergie__. Soudain il dit : « Bonjour les jeunes, est-ce que le café vous donne (gives you) **des __allergies__ ? » Les jeunes disent que non et ils prennent tous un café ensemble. Nicolas commence immédiatement à parler de ses nouvelles __technologies__ médicales et demande à Philippe s'il étudie la __radiologie__. Philippe dit qu'il n'a jamais étudié** (he never studied) **la __radiologie__ mais qu'il a fait un an** (he did one year) **de __biologie__. Nicolas demande à Marie si elle étudie la __psychologie__. Quand elle dit que non, Nicolas dit : « Alors, tu étudies la __météorologie__ ? » Marie regarde Philippe ; il comprend rapidement ce que « différent » veut dire.**

1. Est-ce que Nicolas est paresseux (lazy), ou est-ce qu'il a beaucoup d'énergie ?

2. Est-ce que le café donne des allergies aux jeunes ?

3. De quoi parle Nicolas ?

4. Est-ce que Philippe étudie la radiologie ?

5. Est-ce que Marie étudie la psychologie ?

Chapter 11

English words ending in "–ic" often correspond to "–ique" in French.

French words ending in "–ique" are often adjectives. For example,

an <u>electronic</u> dictionary = *un dictionnaire <u>électronique</u>*

ENGLISH . . . . FRENCH

*All words and phrases in bold are on **Track 11** of the accompanying CD.*

academic . . . . académique
acoustic . . . . acoustique
acrobatic . . . . acrobatique
acrylic . . . . acrylique
Adriatic . . . . Adriatique
aeronautic . . . . aéronautique
aesthetic . . . . esthétique
agnostic . . . . agnostique
alcoholic . . . . **alcoolique** *(for a cocktail, use "alcoolisé")*
algebraic . . . . algébrique
allergic . . . . **allergique**
alphabetic . . . . alphabétique
anachronistic . . . . anachronique
anemic . . . . anémique
analgesic . . . . analgésique
analytic . . . . analytique
anarchic . . . . anarchique
angelic . . . . angélique
anorexic . . . . anorexique
antarctic . . . . antarctique
antibiotic . . . . antibiotique
antique . . . . antique *(only an adjective)*
antiseptic . . . . antiseptique

apathetic	apathique
apocalyptic.	apocalyptique
aquatic.	aquatique
archaic.	archaïque
arctic	arctique
aristocratic	aristocratique
arithmetic	arithmétique
aromatic.	aromatique
arthritic	arthritique
artistic	**artistique** *(more commonly "artiste," for people)*
Asiatic	asiatique
asthmatic	asthmatique
astronomic	astronomique
athletic.	**athlétique**
"I'm very athletic."	**« Je suis très athlétique. »**
Atlantic	Atlantique
atmospheric	atmosphérique
atomic	atomique
authentic	**authentique**
autistic	autistique *(more commonly "autiste," for people)*
autobiographic	autobiographique
automatic	automatique
ballistic.	balistique
balsamic.	balsamique
Baltic	Baltique
barometric	barométrique
basic	basique
biographic	biographique
bionic	bionique
botanic.	botanique
bubonic	bubonique
bucolic.	bucolique
bulimic.	boulimique

bureaucratic . . . . bureautique

caloric . . . . calorique
catastrophic . . . . catastrophique
cathartic . . . . cathartique
Catholic . . . . **Catholique** *(lower case if adjective)*
caustic . . . . caustique
celtic . . . . celtique
ceramic . . . . céramique
characteristic . . . . caractéristique
charismatic . . . . charismatique
choleric . . . . colérique
chronic . . . . **chronique**
cinematic . . . . cinématographique
citric . . . . citrique
civic . . . . civique
classic . . . . **classique**
cleric . . . . ecclésiastique
climatic . . . . climatique
clinic . . . . clinique
comic . . . . comique
concentric . . . . concentrique
cosmetic . . . . cosmétique
cosmic . . . . cosmique
critic . . . . critique *(also used for "criticism"*
and "critical")
cubic . . . . cubique
cylindric . . . . cylindrique
cynic . . . . cynique
cyrillic . . . . cyrillique

democratic . . . . **démocratique**
demographic . . . . démographique
despotic . . . . despotique
diabetic . . . . diabétique
diabolic . . . . diabolique

diagnostic . . . . diagnostique
dialectic . . . . dialectique
didactic . . . . didactique
diplomatic . . . . diplomatique
dogmatic . . . . dogmatique
domestic . . . . **domestique** *(for politics and travel,*
use "intérieur")

Doric . . . . dorique
dramatic . . . . dramatique
drastic . . . . **drastique**
dynamic . . . . dynamique
dyslexic . . . . dyslexique

eccentric . . . . excentrique
ecclesiastic . . . . ecclésiastique
eclectic . . . . éclectique
economic . . . . économique
ecstatic . . . . extatique
egocentric . . . . égocentrique
elastic . . . . élastique
electric . . . . électrique
electromagnetic . . . . électromagnétique
electronic . . . . **électronique**
    "She has an   **« Elle a un**
    electronic dictionary." . . . . **dictionnaire électronique. »**
emblematic . . . . emblématique
emphatic . . . . emphatique
energetic . . . . énergique
enigmatic . . . . énigmatique
epic . . . . épique
epidemic . . . . épidémique
epileptic . . . . épileptique
erotic . . . . érotique
erratic . . . . erratique *(more commonly "imprévisible")*
esoteric . . . . ésotérique
ethic . . . . éthique

ethnic . . . . ethnique
euphoric . . . . euphorique
evangelic . . . . évangélique
exotic . . . . **exotique**
   "I like exotic fruit." . . . . **« J'aime les fruits exotiques. »**

fanatic . . . . fanatique
fantastic . . . . **fantastique**
frenetic . . . . frénétique

gastric . . . . gastrique
geographic . . . . géographique
geologic . . . . géologique
geometric . . . . géométrique
generic . . . . générique
genetic . . . . génétique
geriatric . . . . gériatrique
Germanic . . . . germanique
gothic . . . . gothique

harmonic . . . . harmonique
hedonistic . . . . hédonistique *(more commonly*
                          "hedoniste," for people)
hemispheric . . . . hémisphérique
heretic . . . . hérétique
hermetic . . . . hermétique
heroic . . . . **héroïque**
hierarchic . . . . hiérarchique
hieroglyphic . . . . hiéroglyphique
Hispanic . . . . Hispanique *(only used for*
                         Central/South America,
                         lower case if adjective)
historic . . . . **historique**
   "It's a historic date." . . . . **« C'est une date historique. »**
homeopathic . . . . homéopathique
hydraulic . . . . hydraulique

hygienic	hygiénique
hyperbolic	hyperbolique
hypnotic	hypnotique
hypodermic	hypodermique
hysteric	hystérique
idiomatic	idiomatique
idyllic	idyllique
intrinsic	intrinsèque
ionic	ionique
ironic	**ironique**
"It's ironic!"	**« C'est ironique ! »**
Islamic	islamique
isometric	isométrique
italic	italique
Jurassic	jurassique
kinetic	cinétique
laconic	laconique
lactic	lactique
lethargic	léthargique
linguistic	linguistique
lithographic	lithographique
logic	**logique** (also used for "logical")
logistic	logistique
lunatic	lunatique (meaning "moody," or "spaced-out")
lyric	lyrique
magic	magique (only an adjective, noun is "magie")
magnetic	magnétique
mathematic	mathématique(s)
melodramatic	mélodramatique

metalinguistic . . . . métalinguistique
metallic . . . . métallique
metaphoric . . . . métaphorique
metaphysic . . . . métaphysique
methodic . . . . méthodique
metric. . . . . **métrique**
    "France uses   **« La France utilise**
    the metric system." . . . . **le système métrique. »**
microscopic. . . . . **microscopique**
misanthropic . . . . misanthropique
monarchic . . . . monarchique
mosaic . . . . mosaïque
mnemonic. . . . . mnémotechnique
music . . . . musique
mystic . . . . mystique
mythic . . . . mythique

narcissistic . . . . narcissique
narcotic . . . . narcotique
Nordic . . . . nordique
nostalgic. . . . . **nostalgique**
    "He's very nostalgic." . . . . . . **« Il est très nostalgique. »**
numeric . . . . numérique

oceanic . . . . océanique
olympic . . . . olympique
optic . . . . optique
organic . . . . organique
orgasmic . . . . orgasmique
orthopedic . . . . orthopédique

Pacific . . . . Pacifique
pancreatic . . . . pancréatique
panic . . . . **panique**
panoramic . . . . panoramique
paraplegic . . . . paraplégique

pathetic	**pathétique**
pathologic	pathologique
patriotic	**patriotique**
periodic	périodique
phallic	phallique
philanthropic.	philanthropique
phonetic.	phonétique
photogenic	photogénique
photographic	photographique
picnic.	pique-nique
plastic	plastique
platonic	platonique
pneumatic.	pneumatique
poetic.	**poétique**
polemic	polémique
politic.	politique *(only a noun, "policy"*
	or "politics")
pornographic	pornographique
pragmatic.	pragmatique
prehistoric	préhistorique
problematic	problématique
prolific	prolifique
prophetic	prophétique
prosaic.	prosaïque
prosthetic	prothétique
psychedelic.	psychédélique
psychiatric	psychiatrique
psychic.	psychique
psychotic	psychotique
relic.	relique
republic	république
rhetoric	rhétorique
rhythmic.	rythmique
romantic.	**romantique**
"It's a romantic story."	**« C'est une histoire romantique. »**

rubric	rubrique *(also used for "newspaper column")*
rustic	rustique
sadistic	sadique
sarcastic	**sarcastique**
sardonic	sardonique
satanic	satanique
satiric	satirique
skeptic	sceptique
schematic	schématique
scholastic	scolastique
scientific	**scientifique**
seismic	sismique
semantic	sémantique
sociolinguistic	sociolinguistique
soporific	soporifique
spasmodic	spasmodique
specific	**spécifique**
sporadic	sporadique
static	statique
statistic	statistique
stoic	stoïque
strategic	**stratégique**
stylistic	stylistique
supersonic	supersonique
symbolic	**symbolique**
symmetric	symétrique
sympathetic	sympathique
synthetic	synthétique
tactic	tactique
telegenic	télégénique
telegraphic	télégraphique
telepathic	télépathique

telescopic . . . . télescopique
thematic . . . . thématique
theocratic . . . . théocratique
theoretic . . . . théorique
therapeutic . . . . thérapeutique
tonic . . . . tonique
toxic . . . . toxique
tragic . . . . tragique
traumatic . . . . traumatique
tropic . . . . tropique

ultrasonic . . . . ultrasonique

volcanic . . . . volcanique

zoologic . . . . zoologique

11A.

Reliez les paires de mots synonymes ou associés.

1. stratégique	sarcastique
2. électronique	date
3. artistique	romain
4. classique	créatif
5. ironique	tactique
6. authentique	radio
7. historique	véritable

11B.

Ecoutez et lisez l'histoire. Répondez aux questions suivantes avec des phrases complètes.

Après deux jours à Monaco, Philippe et Marie vont à Nice. Le centre de Nice est très beau, d'une beauté <u>classique</u>. Pendant la journée ils vont visiter quelques musées <u>artistiques</u> et, le soir, ils voient (they see) **que la ville est <u>magique</u>. Il n'y a pas de raison <u>spécifique</u>, mais Nice est une ville <u>fantastique</u>. Philippe conduit une voiture de location** (a rented car)**, mais il y a beaucoup de circulation. Marie pense que ce n'est pas un plan très <u>stratégique</u>. Elle dit : « Le train est mieux** (is better)**, ce n'est pas très <u>romantique</u> de passer les vacances en voiture. » Philippe répond : « On va voir…. »**

1. Quel type de musées visitent-ils ?

2. Quand est-ce que Nice est magique ?

3. Quel type de ville est Nice ?

4. Quel est le problème quand Philippe conduit ?

5. Selon Marie, qu'est-ce qui n'est pas très romantique ?

-ical/-ique

Many English words ending in "–ical" correspond to "–ique" in French.

French words ending in "–ique" are often adjectives. For example,

a <u>botanical</u> garden = *un jardin <u>botanique</u>*

ENGLISH . . . . FRENCH

All words and phrases in bold are on **Track 12** *of the accompanying CD.*

aeronautical . . . . aéronautique
allegorical . . . . allégorique
alphabetical . . . . **alphabétique**
analytical . . . . analytique
anarchical . . . . anarchique
anatomical . . . . anatomique
angelical . . . . angélique
anthropological . . . . anthropologique
antithetical . . . . antithétique
apolitical . . . . apolitique
archaeological . . . . **archéologique**
astrological . . . . astrologique
astronomical . . . . astronomique
asymmetrical . . . . asymétrique
atypical . . . . atypique
autobiographical . . . . autobiographique

biblical . . . . biblique
bibliographical . . . . bibliographique
biochemical . . . . biochimique
biographical . . . . biographique
biological . . . . **biologique**
botanical . . . . **botanique**

"I visited the   **« J'ai visité le**
     botanical gardens.". . . . . . . **jardin botanique. »**

categorical . . . . catégorique
chemical. . . . . chimique
chronological . . . . chronologique
classical . . . . classique
clinical . . . . clinique
comical . . . . comique *(also used for "comedian")*
cosmological. . . . . cosmologique
critical . . . . **critique** *(also used for "critic" and*
                                    "criticism")
cyclical. . . . . cyclique
cylindrical. . . . . cylindrique
cynical . . . . **cynique**
"Don't be cynical!" . . . . **« Ne sois pas cynique ! »**

diabolical. . . . . diabolique
dialectical. . . . . dialectique

ecclesiastical. . . . . ecclésiastique
ecological. . . . . écologique
economical. . . . . économique
electrical. . . . . **électrique**
empirical . . . . empirique
ethical . . . . éthique
evangelical. . . . . évangélique

fanatical. . . . . fanatique

genealogical. . . . . généalogique
geographical . . . . géographique
geological . . . . géologique
geometrical. . . . . géométrique

hierarchical . . . . hiérarchique

historical . . . . historique
hypothetical . . . . hypothétique
hysterical . . . . hystérique

identical . . . . **identique**
 "The twins   **« Les jumeaux**
  are identical." . . . . **sont identiques. »**
ideological . . . . idéologique
illogical . . . . illogique
ironical. . . . . ironique

logical . . . . **logique**
logistical. . . . . logistique
lyrical. . . . . lyrique

magical . . . . **magique**
mathematical . . . . mathématique
mechanical. . . . . mécanique
metaphorical. . . . . métaphorique
metaphysical. . . . . métaphysique
meteorological . . . . météorologique
methodical . . . . méthodique
mystical . . . . mystique
mythical . . . . mythique
mythological . . . . mythologique

nautical . . . . nautique
neurological . . . . neurologique
numerical . . . . numérique

obstetrical. . . . . obstétrique
optical . . . . optique

pathological . . . . pathologique
pedagogical. . . . . pédagogique
periodical. . . . . périodique

pharmaceutical . . . . pharmaceutique
philosophical . . . . philosophique
physical . . . . physique
physiological . . . . physiologique
political . . . . politique
practical . . . . **pratique**
problematical . . . . problématique
psychological . . . . psychologique

rhetorical . . . . rhétorique
rhythmical . . . . rythmique

sabbatical . . . . sabbatique
satirical . . . . satirique
sociological . . . . sociologique
sociopolitical . . . . sociopolitique
spherical . . . . sphérique
statistical . . . . statistique
symbolical . . . . symbolique
symmetrical . . . . symétrique

tactical . . . . tactique
technical . . . . **technique** *(also used for "technique")*
technological . . . . technologique
theological . . . . théologique
theoretical . . . . théorique
typical . . . . **typique**
   "That's typical!" . . . . **« C'est typique ! »**
typographical . . . . typographique
tyrannical . . . . tyrannique

zoological . . . . zoologique

12A.

Reliez les paires de mots synonymes ou associés.

1. typique   humain
2. botanique   moralité
3. pratique   mystique
4. électrique   jardin
5. éthique   lampe
6. biologique   normal
7. magique   rationnel

12B.

Ecoutez et lisez l'histoire. Répondez aux questions suivantes avec des phrases complètes.

Philippe dit : « C'est si beau Nice que nous pouvons passer le mois entier (the whole month) **ici. » Marie comprend mais elle dit : « Non, j'ai l'esprit <u>pratique</u>, nous devons continuer notre voyage de façon <u>logique</u>** (logical manner). **» Philippe voit qu'elle est très <u>logique</u> maintenant et dit : « Marie, c'est <u>typique</u>, j'admire ton sens <u>pratique</u> ! » Elle répond : « Ne sois pas si <u>critique</u> ! Toi aussi tu veux aller à Marseille, pas vrai ? » Philippe répond : « Tu as raison** (you're right), **allons à Marseille ! »**

1. Est-ce que Philippe veut rester à Nice ou partir ?

2. De quelle façon Marie veut-elle voyager ?

3. Est-ce que Marie a le sens pratique ?

4. Où est-ce qu'ils vont maintenant ?

5. Que dit Marie de Marseille ?

-id/-ide

Many English words ending in "–id" correspond to "–ide" in French.

French words ending in "–ide" are usually adjectives. For example,

a <u>humid</u> day = *un jour <u>humide</u>*

ENGLISH . . . . FRENCH	

*All words and phrases in bold are on **Track 13** of the accompanying CD.*

acid . . . . acide
antacid . . . . antiacide
arid . . . . aride
avid . . . . avide

candid . . . . candide *(meaning "innocent," "naïve")*
Cupid . . . . cupide

fluid . . . . fluide
frigid . . . . frigide

humid . . . . **humide**
     "Today is very humid." . . . . . **« Aujourd'hui il fait très humide. »**
hybrid . . . . hybride

insipid . . . . insipide
intrepid . . . . intrépide
invalid . . . . invalide *(meaning "disabled soldier/worker")*

liquid . . . . **liquide**
livid . . . . livide
lucid . . . . lucide

morbid . . . . morbide

placid . . . . placide
putrid . . . . putride

rapid . . . . **rapide**
rigid . . . . **rigide**

solid . . . . solide
sordid . . . . sordide
splendid . . . . **splendide**
stupid . . . . **stupide**

timid . . . . **timide**
    "Matthew is very timid." . . . . **« Matthieu est très timide. »**
torrid . . . . torride

valid . . . . **valide**
    "Your opinion is valid." . . . . . **« Ton opinion est valide. »**

13A.

Reliez les paires de mots synonymes ou associés.

1. valide   inflexible
2. rigide   réservé
3. acide   idiot
4. liquide   magnifique
5. timide   vrai
6. stupide   citron
7. splendide   fluide

13B.

Ecoutez et lisez l'histoire. Répondez aux questions suivantes avec des phrases complètes.

Pour aller à Marseille, Philippe et Marie décident de louer (rent) **une autre voiture. Marie dit que c'est un plan <u>stupide</u>, mais Philippe pense que c'est un plan <u>splendide</u>. Marie dit : « Mais à Nice, le voyage n'était pas très <u>rapide</u>.... » Philippe dit qu'il préfère conduire quand il fait chaud. Pendant le voyage il fait très <u>humide</u> et, soudain, Philippe devient très pâle et il a mal au ventre** (stomachache). **Marie ne dit rien et va dans une pharmacie acheter un peu d'<u>antiacide</u> pour Philippe. Le pharmacien dit qu'il doit** (he must) **boire beaucoup de <u>liquide</u> et ne pas manger de nourriture <u>acide</u>.**

1. Que dit Marie du plan d'aller à Marseille en voiture ?

2. Que pense Philippe de son idée ?

3. Quel temps fait-il pendant le voyage ?

4. Le pharmacien dit qu'il doit boire quoi ?

5. Le pharmacien dit qu'il ne doit pas manger quoi ?

-ism/-isme

English words ending in "– ism" often correspond to "– isme" in French.

French words ending in "–isme" are usually nouns. For example,

communism = *le communisme*

ENGLISH . . . . FRENCH

All words and phrases in bold are on **Track 14** *of the accompanying CD.*

activism . . . . activisme
absenteeism . . . . absentéisme
absolutism . . . . absolutisme
alcoholism . . . . **alcoolisme**
   "Alcoholism is dangerous." . . . **« L'alcoolisme est dangereux. »**
altruism . . . . altruisme
Americanism. . . . . américanisme
anachronism . . . . anachronisme
anarchism. . . . . anarchisme
anglicism . . . . anglicisme
antagonism. . . . . antagonisme
anthropomorphism. . . . . anthropomorphisme
antifascism . . . . **antifascisme**
antiracism. . . . . antiracisme
anti-Semitism. . . . . antisémitisme
aphorism . . . . aphorisme
astigmatism. . . . . astigmatisme
atheism . . . . athéisme
athleticism . . . . **athlétisme**
autism . . . . autisme

behaviorism . . . . behaviorisme
bilingualism . . . . bilinguisme

botulism	botulisme
Buddhism	bouddhisme
cannibalism	cannibalisme
capitalism	**capitalisme**
catechism	catéchisme
Catholicism	catholicisme
centralism	centralisme
chauvinism	chauvinisme
classicism	classicisme
colonialism	colonialisme
communism	**communisme**

"Communism is a
political movement." . . . . **« Le communisme est un
mouvement politique. »**

conservatism	conservatisme
cubism	cubisme
cynicism	cynisme
Darwinism	darwinisme
deism	déisme
despotism	despotisme
determinism	déterminisme
dogmatism	dogmatisme
dualism	dualisme
dynamism	dynamisme
egoism	égoïsme *(meaning "selfishness")*
elitism	élitisme
eroticism	érotisme
euphemism	euphémisme
existentialism	existentialisme
exorcism	exorcisme
expansionism	expansionnisme
expressionism	expressionnisme
extremism	extrémisme

fanaticism	fanatisme
fascism	**fascisme**
fatalism	fatalisme
favoritism	favoritisme
federalism	fédéralisme
feminism	**féminisme**
formalism	formalisme
fundamentalism	fondamentalisme
futurism	futurisme
globalism	globalisme
hedonism	hédonisme
heroism	héroïsme
Hinduism	hindouisme
humanism	humanisme
hypnotism	hypnotisme
idealism	idéalisme
imperialism	impérialisme
impressionism	**impressionnisme**

"Impressionism is an   **« L'impressionnisme est un**
artistic movement."   **mouvement artistique. »**

individualism	individualisme
industrialism	industrialisme
internationalism	internationalisme
isolationism	isolationnisme
journalism	journalisme
Judaism	judaïsme
legalism	légalisme
Leninism	léninisme
liberalism	libéralisme
lyricism	lyrisme

magnetism	magnétisme
Marxism	marxisme
masochism	masochisme
mechanism	**mécanisme**
metabolism	métabolisme
microorganism	microorganisme
minimalism	minimalisme
modernism	modernisme
monotheism	monothéisme
moralism	moralisme
narcissism	narcissisme
nationalism	**nationalisme**
naturalism	naturalisme
Nazism	nazisme
neoclassicism	néoclassicisme
neofascism	néofascisme
neologism	néologisme
nepotism	népotisme
nihilism	nihilisme
nonconformism	non-conformisme
nudism	nudisme
objectivism	objectivisme
opportunism	opportunisme
optimism	**optimisme**

"Optimism is a good thing." . . . . **« L'optimisme est une bonne chose. »**

organism	**organisme**
parallelism	parallélisme
patriotism	patriotisme
perfectionism	perfectionnisme
pessimism	pessimisme
pluralism	pluralisme
polytheism	polythéisme
populism	populisme

positivism . . . . positivisme
postmodernism . . . . postmodernisme
pragmatism. . . . . pragmatisme
primitivism . . . . primitivisme
prism . . . . prisme
professionalism . . . . **professionnalisme**
protectionism . . . . protectionnisme
provincialism. . . . . provincialisme
purism . . . . purisme
puritanism. . . . . puritanisme

racism . . . . **racisme**
   "Racism is intolerable." . . . . . **« Le racisme est intolérable. »**
radicalism. . . . . radicalisme
rationalism . . . . rationalisme
realism. . . . . réalisme
regionalism. . . . . régionalisme
relativism . . . . relativisme
ritualism . . . . ritualisme
romanticism . . . . romantisme

sadism . . . . sadisme
satanism. . . . . satanisme
skepticism. . . . . scepticisme
schism . . . . schisme
sensualism . . . . sensualisme
separatism . . . . séparatisme
sexism . . . . sexisme
socialism . . . . **socialisme**
spiritualism . . . . spiritualisme
Stalinism. . . . . stalinisme
structuralism . . . . structuralisme
surrealism. . . . . surréalisme
syllogism . . . . syllogisme
symbolism. . . . . symbolisme

terrorism	**terrorisme**
totalitarianism	totalitarisme
tourism	**tourisme**
"There's a lot of	« **Il y a beaucoup de**
tourism in France."	**tourisme en France.** »
truism	truisme
vandalism	vandalisme
verbalism	verbalisme
voyeurism	voyeurisme

14A.

Reliez les paires de mots synonymes ou associés.

1. communisme	Karl Marx
2. optimisme	patriotisme
3. impressionisme	bombe
4. féminisme	passeport
5. nationalisme	positif
6. tourisme	femme
7. terrorisme	art

14B.

Ecoutez et lisez l'histoire. Répondez aux questions suivantes avec des phrases complètes.

Après le premier jour à Marseille, Philippe se sent mieux (feels better)**. Il y a beaucoup de <u>tourisme</u> à Marseille et beaucoup d'histoire, mais ils décident de se reposer quelques jours sur la plage. Marie achète un livre sur l'histoire de France qui parle de l'influence du <u>socialisme</u>, du <u>fascisme</u>, et du <u>communisme</u> en France. Le livre décrit le <u>nationalisme</u> français et Marie demande à Philippe ce qu'il pense du** (what he thinks about) **<u>capitalisme</u>. Philippe dit : « Marie, tout ça c'est très intéressant, mais... mangeons une glace** (let's get an ice cream) **! »**

1. Est-ce qu'il y a beaucoup de tourisme à Marseille ?

2. Le livre parle de l'influence de quoi en France ?

3. Que décrit le livre ?

4. Qu'est-ce que Marie demande à Philippe ?

5. Que dit Philippe à la fin ?

Chapter 15   -ist/-iste

Many English words ending in "–ist" correspond to "–iste" in French.

French words ending in "–iste" are usually nouns. For example,

an artist = *un/une artiste*

ENGLISH . . . . FRENCH

All words and phrases in bold are on **Track 15** *of the accompanying CD.*

abolitionist . . . . abolitionniste
activist . . . . activiste
alarmist . . . . alarmiste
alchemist . . . . alchimiste
altruist . . . . altruiste
anarchist . . . . anarchiste
anatomist . . . . anatomiste
anesthesiologist. . . . . anesthésiste
antagonist . . . . antagoniste
anthropologist. . . . . anthropologiste
archivist . . . . archiviste *(also used for "filing clerk")*
artist . . . . **artiste**
    "Monet is an incredible artist." . . . **« Monet est un artiste incroyable. »**

Baptist . . . . Baptiste
bassist . . . . bassiste
behaviorist . . . . behavioriste
biologist. . . . . biologiste
botanist . . . . botaniste
Buddhist. . . . . bouddhiste *(uppercase if referring to a person)*

Calvinist . . . . calviniste *(uppercase if referring to a person)*

capitalist . . . . **capitaliste**

caricaturist . . . . caricaturiste

cellist . . . . violoncelliste

centralist . . . . centraliste

chemist . . . . chimiste

colonialist . . . . colonialiste

communist . . . . **communiste**

conformist . . . . conformiste

cubist . . . . cubiste

cyclist . . . . cycliste

dentist . . . . **dentiste**
    "I'm afraid of the dentist." . . . **« J'ai peur du dentiste. »**

ecologist . . . . écologiste

economist . . . . économiste

egotist . . . . égoïste

elitist . . . . élitiste

essayist . . . . essayiste

exhibitionist . . . . exhibitionniste

existentialist . . . . existentialiste

exorcist . . . . exorciste

expansionist . . . . expansionniste

extremist . . . . extrémiste

fascist . . . . fasciste

fatalist . . . . fataliste

federalist . . . . fédéraliste

feminist . . . . féministe

finalist . . . . **finaliste**

florist . . . . **fleuriste**
    "I'm going to the florist." . . . . **« Je vais chez le fleuriste. »**

flutist . . . . flûtiste

formalist . . . . formaliste

fundamentalist. . . . . fondamentaliste
futurist . . . . futuriste

guitarist . . . . **guitariste**

harpist . . . . harpiste
hedonist . . . . hédoniste
humanist. . . . . humaniste

idealist. . . . . **idéaliste**
illusionist . . . . illusionniste
imperialist. . . . . impérialiste
impressionist . . . . impressionniste
individualist . . . . individualiste
isolationist . . . . isolationniste

journalist . . . . journaliste
jurist. . . . . juriste

Leninist. . . . . léniniste *(uppercase if referring
to a person)*
list . . . . **liste**
lobbyist . . . . lobbyiste
loyalist . . . . loyaliste

machinist . . . . machiniste
Marxist. . . . . marxiste *(uppercase if referring
to a person)*
masochist . . . . masochiste
materialist. . . . . matérialiste
Methodist . . . . méthodiste *(uppercase if referring
to a person)*
minimalist. . . . . **minimaliste**
modernist . . . . moderniste
monopolist . . . . monopoliste
moralist . . . . moraliste

nationalist. . . . . nationaliste

naturalist . . . . naturaliste

nihilist . . . . nihiliste

nonconformist . . . . non-conformiste

novelist. . . . . nouvelliste *(meaning "short-story writer")*

nudist. . . . . nudiste

nutritionist . . . . **nutritionniste**

objectivist . . . . objectiviste

optimist . . . . **optimiste**

   "She's an optimist." . . . . **« Elle est optimiste. »**

opportunist . . . . opportuniste

organist . . . . organiste

pacifist. . . . . pacifiste

perfectionist . . . . perfectionniste

pessimist . . . . **pessimiste**

pianist . . . . **pianiste**

   "My father is a pianist." . . . . . **« Mon père est pianiste. »**

pluralist . . . . pluraliste

populist . . . . populiste

positivist . . . . positiviste

pragmatist . . . . pragmatiste

prohibitionist. . . . . prohibitionniste

protagonist . . . . protagoniste

purist . . . . puriste

racist . . . . **raciste**

realist. . . . . **réaliste**

   "This woman is a realist." . . . **« Cette femme est réaliste. »**

receptionist. . . . . réceptionniste

reformist. . . . . réformiste

sadomasochist. . . . . sadomasochiste

secessionist. . . . . sécessionniste

semifinalist . . . . demi-finaliste

separatist . . . . séparatiste

sexist . . . . sexiste

socialist . . . . socialiste

soloist . . . . soliste

specialist . . . . spécialiste

spiritualist . . . . spiritualiste

structuralist . . . . structuraliste

stylist . . . . styliste

surrealist . . . . surréaliste

symbolist . . . . symboliste

terrorist . . . . **terroriste**

tourist . . . . **touriste**

zoologist . . . . zoologiste

15A.

Reliez les paires de mots synonymes ou associés.

1. artiste	visiteur
2. touriste	peintre
3. pessimiste	compétition
4. optimiste	bouquet
5. dentiste	négatif
6. finaliste	dent
7. fleuriste	positif

15B.

Ecoutez et lisez l'histoire. Répondez aux questions suivantes avec des phrases complètes.

Destination : Montpellier ! Pendant que Philippe et Marie se promènent dans Montpellier ils rencontrent (they meet) **un autre couple de Strasbourg. Le jeune homme est <u>dentiste</u> et la jeune femme est <u>artiste</u>. Les nouveaux amis de Philippe et Marie sont des <u>touristes</u> « professionnels » : ils voyagent beaucoup et ils savent beaucoup de choses** (they know a lot) **sur Montpellier. Marie a une <u>liste</u> de questions et le <u>dentiste</u> peut donner une réponse à chaque question. Ils sont très intelligents mais ils forment un couple étrange** (a strange couple)**. La jeune femme est <u>optimiste</u> alors que son petit ami est <u>pessimiste</u>. Elle est <u>idéaliste</u> et il est <u>réaliste</u>. Le <u>dentiste</u> dit à Philippe et Marie : « Vous voulez aller à Perpignan avec nous ? » Philippe répond : « On va voir…. »**

1. Que fait le jeune homme qu'ils rencontrent ?

2. Est-ce que les nouveaux amis de Philippe et Marie voyagent souvent (often) ?

3. Marie a une liste de quoi ?

4. Comment est le dentiste ?

5. Comment est l'artiste ?

Chapter 16

English words ending in "–ive" often correspond to "–if " in French.

French words ending in "–if" are usually adjectives. For example,

a <u>creative</u> artist = *un artiste <u>créatif</u>*

If the French adjective is feminine it will end in "–ive," just like the English. For example,

a <u>creative</u> woman = *une femme <u>creative</u>*

ENGLISH . . . . FRENCH

*All words and phrases in bold are on **Track 16** of the accompanying CD.*

abrasive. . . . . abrasif
abusive . . . . abusif
accusative . . . . accusatif
active. . . . . **actif**
   "My friend is active." . . . . . . **« Mon ami est actif. »**
additive . . . . additif
adhesive. . . . . adhésif
adjective. . . . . **adjectif**
   "*Cute* is an adjective.". . . . . . **« *Mignon* est un adjectif. »**
administrative . . . . administratif
adoptive. . . . . adoptif
affective . . . . affectif
affirmative . . . . affirmatif
aggressive . . . . **agressif**
allusive. . . . . allusif
alternative . . . . alternatif
associative . . . . associatif
attentive . . . . attentif

attractive . . . . attractif *(more commonly "attrayant" or "attirant")*

captive . . . . captif
cognitive . . . . cognitif
cohesive . . . . cohésif
collective . . . . collectif
combative . . . . combatif
commemorative . . . . commémoratif
communicative . . . . communicatif
comparative . . . . comparatif
competitive . . . . **compétitif**
comprehensive . . . . compréhensif *(also used for "understanding")*

compulsive . . . . compulsif
connective . . . . conjonctif
consecutive . . . . **consécutif**
constructive . . . . constructif
contemplative . . . . contemplatif
contraceptive . . . . contraceptif
convulsive . . . . convulsif
cooperative . . . . **coopératif**
corrective . . . . correctif
corrosive . . . . corrosif
creative . . . . **créatif**
"This artist is creative." . . . . . **« Cet artiste est créatif. »**
cumulative . . . . cumulatif
curative . . . . curatif
cursive . . . . cursif *(only used in feminine form, "cursive")*

dative . . . . datif
decisive . . . . décisif
declarative . . . . déclaratif
decorative . . . . décoratif
deductive . . . . déductif

defensive . . . . défensif
definitive . . . . **définitif**
degenerative. . . . . dégénératif
demonstrative . . . . démonstratif
depressive . . . . dépressif
descriptive . . . . descriptif
destructive . . . . **destructif**
digestive. . . . . digestif
diminutive. . . . . diminutif
directive . . . . directif *(only used in feminine form,*
"directive")
discursive . . . . discursif
distinctive . . . . distinctif

effective . . . . effectif
elective. . . . . électif
evasive. . . . . évasif
excessive . . . . **excessif**
exclusive . . . . exclusif
executive . . . . **exécutif** *(more commonly "cadre")*
exhaustive . . . . exhaustif
expansive. . . . . expansif
expletive. . . . . explétif *(more commonly "juron,"*
for "swear word")
explosive . . . . explosif
expressive . . . . expressif
extensive . . . . extensif

figurative . . . . figuratif *(more commonly "figuré")*
fugitive. . . . . fugitif
furtive. . . . . furtif

genitive . . . . génitif

hyperactive. . . . . hyperactif

imaginative. . . . . **imaginatif**
imitative . . . . imitatif
imperative . . . . impératif
implosive . . . . implosif
impulsive . . . . impulsif
inactive . . . . inactif
incisive. . . . . incisif
indicative . . . . indicatif
infinitive . . . . infinitif
inoffensive . . . . inoffensif
instinctive . . . . instinctif
instructive . . . . instructif
intensive. . . . . intensif
interactive. . . . . **interactif**
interrogative . . . . interrogatif
intransitive . . . . intransitif
introspective . . . . introspectif
intuitive . . . . intuitif
inventive. . . . . inventif

laxative . . . . laxatif
legislative. . . . . législatif
lucrative . . . . lucratif

massive . . . . massif *(also used for "solid")*
meditative. . . . . méditatif
motive . . . . motif
multiplicative. . . . . multiplicatif

narrative. . . . . narratif *(also used for "narration")*
native. . . . . natif
negative . . . . **négatif**
nominative . . . . nominatif

objective. . . . . **objectif**
offensive . . . . **offensif**

oppressive . . . . oppressif

partitive . . . . partitif

passive . . . . passif

pejorative . . . . péjoratif

pensive . . . . pensif

perceptive . . . . perceptif *(more commonly "perspicace")*

permissive . . . . permissif

persuasive . . . . persuasif

plaintive . . . . plaintif

positive . . . . **positif**

possessive . . . . **possessif**

preparative . . . . préparatif

preservative . . . . préservatif *(meaning "condom")*

preventive . . . . préventif

primitive . . . . **primitif**

productive . . . . **productif**

progressive . . . . progressif

prohibitive . . . . prohibitif

punitive . . . . punitif

qualitative . . . . qualitatif

quantitative . . . . quantitatif

radioactive . . . . radioactif

reactive . . . . réactif

receptive . . . . réceptif

recessive . . . . récessif

regressive . . . . régressif

relative . . . . relatif *(only an adjective)*

repetitive . . . . **répétitif**

    "This movie is repetitive." . . . . **« Ce film est répétitif. »**

representative . . . . représentatif *(only an adjective)*

repressive . . . . répressif

respective . . . . respectif

reproductive . . . . reproductif

repulsive. . . . . répulsif

restrictive . . . . restrictif

retroactive . . . . rétroactif

retrospective . . . . rétrospectif *(only an adjective)*

sedative . . . . sédatif

selective . . . . **sélectif**

speculative . . . . spéculatif

subjective . . . . **subjectif**

subjunctive . . . . subjonctif

substantive . . . . substantif

subversive. . . . . subversif

successive. . . . . successif

suggestive. . . . . suggestif

superlative . . . . superlatif

transitive. . . . . transitif

unproductive. . . . . improductif

vegetative. . . . . végétatif

16A.

Reliez les paires de mots synonymes ou associés.

1. consécutif	cause
2. créatif	optimiste
3. positif	artistique
4. exécutif	impartial
5. motif	fataliste
6. négatif	successif
7. objectif	patron

16B.

Ecoutez et lisez l'histoire. Répondez aux questions suivantes avec des phrases complètes.

Philippe trouve la ville de Montpellier absolument fascinante. Il avait entendu (he had heard) **des choses <u>négatives</u> sur Montpellier, mais il voit une région <u>créative</u> et <u>compétitive</u>. Marie a aussi une impression <u>positive</u> de Montpellier. Avant de partir Philippe veut aller voir le village où est né** (was born) **son grand-père. « C'est un bon <u>motif</u> pour y aller » dit Marie. Ils vont à Juvignac, un village pas très <u>actif</u> mais très accueillant** (welcoming)**. Ils passent deux jours <u>consécutifs</u> là-bas.**

1. Qu'est-ce que Philippe avait entendu sur Montpellier ?

2. Que pense Philippe de Montpellier ?

3. Quelle est l'impression de Marie sur Montpellier ?

4. Comment est le village de Juvignac ?

5. Combien de jours est-ce qu'ils passent là-bas ?

Chapter 17

English words ending in "–or" often correspond to "–eur" in French.

French words ending in "–eur" are usually nouns. For example,

an error = *une erreur*

ENGLISH . . . . FRENCH

All words and phrases in bold are on **Track 17** *of the accompanying CD.*

accelerator . . . . accélérateur

accumulator . . . . accumulateur

actor . . . . **acteur**

adaptor . . . . adaptateur

administrator. . . . . administrateur

aggressor . . . . agresseur

agitator . . . . agitateur

alternator . . . . alternateur

ambassador . . . . ambassadeur

anterior . . . . antérieur

applicator. . . . . applicateur

ardor . . . . ardeur

auditor . . . . auditeur

author . . . . **auteur**

aviator . . . . aviateur

benefactor . . . . bienfaiteur

calculator . . . . calculateur *(only used for "a calculating person"; for the electronic device, use "calculatrice")*

candor . . . . candeur *(meaning "innocence")*

carburetor. . . . . carburateur

censor . . . . censeur

clamor . . . . clameur

collaborator . . . . collaborateur

collector . . . . collectionneur

color . . . . **couleur**

    "I like this color." . . . . **« J'aime cette couleur. »**

commentator . . . . commentateur

compressor . . . . compresseur

conductor . . . . conducteur *(for music, use "chef d'orchestre")*

confessor . . . . confesseur

conservator . . . . conservateur

conspirator . . . . conspirateur

coordinator . . . . coordinateur

creator . . . . **créateur**

cultivator . . . . cultivateur

cursor . . . . curseur

debtor . . . . débiteur

decorator . . . . décorateur

demonstrator . . . . démonstrateur *(for political demonstrations, use "manifestant")*

detector . . . . détecteur

detonator . . . . détonateur

detractor . . . . détracteur

dictator . . . . **dictateur**

director . . . . **directeur** *(for movies, use "metteur en scene")*

dishonor . . . . déshonneur

distributor . . . . distributeur

divisor . . . . diviseur

doctor . . . . **docteur**

    "I'm going to the doctor." . . . **« Je vais chez le docteur. »**

donor . . . . donateur *(only used in the context of a charity)* editor . . . . éditeur *(also used for "publisher")*

educator . . . . éducateur

elector . . . . électeur

emperor . . . . empereur

equator . . . . équateur

error . . . . **erreur**

    "There is an error." . . . . « **Il y a une erreur.** »

excavator . . . . excavateur

executor . . . . exécuteur

exterior . . . . **extérieur**

factor . . . . facteur *(also used for "postman")*

favor . . . . **faveur**

fervor . . . . ferveur

generator . . . . générateur

gladiator . . . . gladiateur

governor . . . . gouverneur

honor . . . . honneur

horror . . . . **horreur**

    "It's a horror movie." . . . . « **C'est un film d'horreur.** »

humor . . . . humeur *(meaning "mood")*

illustrator . . . . illustrateur

imitator . . . . imitateur

impersonator . . . . imitateur

impostor . . . . imposteur

incinerator . . . . incinérateur

incubator . . . . incubateur

indicator . . . . indicateur

inferior . . . . **inférieur** *(also used for "lower")*

innovator . . . . **innovateur**

inspector . . . . inspecteur

instigator . . . . instigateur

instructor . . . . instructeur

interior . . . . **intérieur**

interlocutor . . . . interlocuteur

interrogator. . . . . interrogateur

interruptor. . . . . interrupteur *(also used for "electrical switch")*

inventor . . . . **inventeur**

investor . . . . investisseur

labor . . . . labeur

languor . . . . langueur

legislator . . . . législateur

liberator . . . . libérateur

liquidator . . . . liquidateur

liquor. . . . . liqueur *(meaning "liqueur")*

major. . . . . majeur *(also used for "over 18 years old")*

manipulator . . . . manipulateur

mediator. . . . . médiateur

minor. . . . . mineur

moderator. . . . . modérateur *(more commonly "animateur")*

monitor . . . . moniteur *(also used for "coach")*

monsignor . . . . monseigneur

motor. . . . . **moteur**

narrator . . . . narrateur

navigator . . . . navigateur

negotiator. . . . . négociateur

odor . . . . **odeur** *(also used for "scent")*

operator. . . . . opérateur

oppressor . . . . oppresseur

orator. . . . . orateur

pallor	pâleur
pastor	pasteur
persecutor	persécuteur
possessor	possesseur
posterior	postérieur
precursor	précurseur
predator	prédateur
predecessor	prédécesseur
professor	**professeur** (also used for "teacher")

"My aunt is a professor." . . . . **« Ma tante est professeur. »**

projector	projecteur
prosecutor	procureur
prospector	prospecteur
protector	**protecteur**

radiator	radiateur
rancor	rancœur
reactor	réacteur
receptor	récepteur
reflector	réflecteur
refrigerator	réfrigérateur
regulator	régulateur
respirator	respirateur
rigor	rigueur
rumor	rumeur (also used for "low noise," "murmur")

savior	sauveur
savor	saveur
sculptor	sculpteur
sector	secteur
selector	sélecteur
semiconductor	semi-conducteur
senator	**sénateur**

"My uncle is a senator." . . . . **« Mon oncle est sénateur. »**

separator	séparateur

simulator . . . . simulateur

solicitor . . . . solliciteur

spectator . . . . spectateur

speculator. . . . . spéculateur

splendor. . . . . splendeur

stupor. . . . . stupeur *(also used for "amazement")*

successor . . . . successeur

superior . . . . supérieur *(also used for "upper")*

tailor . . . . tailleur

terror . . . . **terreur**

torpor. . . . . torpeur

tractor . . . . tracteur

transgressor . . . . transgresseur

translator . . . . traducteur

tumor. . . . . **tumeur**

tutor. . . . . tuteur *(meaning "guardian")*

ulterior . . . . ultérieur *(meaning "subsequent")*

valor . . . . valeur

vendor . . . . vendeur

ventilator . . . . ventilateur *(meaning "electrical fan")*

violator. . . . . violateur

visitor. . . . . visiteur

vapor. . . . . **vapeur** *(also used for "steam")*

17A.

Reliez les paires de mots synonymes ou associés

1. docteur	université
2. acteur	innovateur
3. sénateur	peur
4. professeur	médecin
5. inventeur	voiture
6 moteur	théâtre
7. terreur	congrès

17B.

Ecoutez et lisez l'histoire. Répondez aux questions suivantes avec des phrases complètes.

Dès qu'ils (as soon as) **arrivent à Toulouse, l'oncle leur dit qu'il y aura une fête** (a party) **chez lui ce soir. Marie remarque immédiatement la** <u>terreur</u> **sur le visage de Philippe. Quand ils sont seuls, Philippe dit : « Quelle** <u>erreur</u> **de venir ici ! Fais-moi une** <u>faveur</u> **: dis-moi que je n'ai pas besoin d'aller à cette fête. » Marie ne répond même pas** (doesn't even respond) **et Philippe comprend qu'il doit y aller. La « fête » est très difficile pour Philippe. Toutes les deux minutes, l'oncle dit : « Cet homme est** <u>docteur</u>**, celui-là** (that one) **est** <u>professeur</u>**, l'autre est** <u>inventeur</u>**. » Pendant un moment, Philippe est intéressé quand l'oncle lui dit : « Le** <u>sénateur</u> **va venir avec un** <u>acteur</u> **très célèbre. » Mais l'**<u>acteur</u> **n'est pas célèbre et le** <u>sénateur</u> **est très, très vieux.**

1. Que remarque Marie sur le visage de Philippe ?

2. Que dit Philippe sur la décision d'aller à Toulouse ?

3. Que dit Philippe sur la fête ?

4. Est-ce que l'acteur est célèbre ?

5. Est-ce que le sénateur est jeune ?

-ory/-oire

English words ending in "–ory" generally correspond to "–oire" in French.

French words ending in "–oire" can be nouns or adjectives. For example,

an accessory (n.) = *un accessoire*
contradictory (adj.) = *contradictoire*

ENGLISH . . . . FRENCH

All words and phrases in bold are on **Track 18** *of the accompanying CD.*

accessory . . . . **accessoire**
ambulatory . . . . ambulatoire

circulatory . . . . circulatoire
compensatory . . . . compensatoire
conservatory . . . . conservatoire
contradictory . . . . **contradictoire**
    "That's contradictory!" . . . . . . **« C'est contradictoire ! »**
crematory . . . . crématoire

declaratory . . . . déclaratoire
derisory . . . . dérisoire
derogatory . . . . dérogatoire
discriminatory . . . . discriminatoire

exploratory . . . . exploratoire

glory . . . . gloire

hallucinatory . . . . hallucinatoire
history . . . . histoire

illusory . . . . illusoire
inflammatory . . . . inflammatoire
interrogatory . . . . interrogatoire
ivory . . . . ivoire

laboratory . . . . **laboratoire**
    "She works in a laboratory." . . . **« Elle travaille dans un laboratoire. »**

memory . . . . mémoire
migratory . . . . migratoire

obligatory . . . . **obligatoire**
observatory . . . . observatoire
oratory . . . . oratoire

peremptory . . . . péremptoire
preparatory . . . . préparatoire
promontory . . . . promontoire
purgatory . . . . **purgatoire**

refectory . . . . réfectoire
repertory . . . . répertoire
respiratory . . . . respiratoire

suppository . . . . suppositoire

territory . . . . **territoire**
    "That's his territory." . . . . **« C'est son territoire. »**
trajectory . . . . trajectoire
transitory . . . . transitoire

victory . . . . victoire

18A.

Reliez les paires de mots synonymes ou associés.

1. territoire   nécessaire
2. accessoire   zone
3. contradictoire   gagner
4. laboratoire   éléphant
5. obligatoire   ceinture
6. ivoire   recherche
7. victoire   paradoxal

18B.

Ecoutez et lisez l'histoire. Répondez aux questions suivantes avec des phrases complètes.

Philippe est très content quand ils partent finalement de Toulouse pour Bordeaux. Il dit : « J'aurais préféré (I'd have preferred) **une auberge** (a hostel)**. » Marie admet que c'était une <u>histoire</u> étrange. Philippe dit : « Mais, qu'est-ce que tu dis ? C'était pire que le <u>purgatoire</u> ! » Marie répond : « Tu n'avais pas besoin de** (you didn't have to) **venir, ce n'était pas <u>obligatoire</u>. » Philippe rit de ce commentaire <u>contradictoire</u> mais ne répond pas. Philippe dit : « Alors tu me dois une faveur, pas vrai ? » Marie dit : « On va voir…. »**

1. Où vont-ils après Toulouse ?

2. Qu'est-ce que Philippe aurait préféré ?

3. Philippe dit que la fête était pire que quoi ?

4. Est-il vrai que sa présence n'était pas obligatoire ?

5. Est-ce que Philippe répond au dernier commentaire contradictoire de Marie ?

-ous/-eux

English words ending in "–ous" generally correspond to "–eux" in French.

French words ending in "–eux" are usually adjectives. For example,

a <u>delicious</u> dinner = *un dîner <u>délicieux</u>*

If the French adjective is feminine, it will end in "–euse." For example,

a <u>delicious</u> pie = une tarte <u>délicieuse</u>

ENGLISH . . . . FRENCH

All words and phrases in bold are on **Track 19** *of the accompanying CD.*

advantageous . . . . avantageux

adventurous . . . . aventureux

ambitious . . . . **ambitieux**

    "My brother is ambitious." . . . **« Mon frère est ambitieux. »**

amorous . . . . amoureux

aqueous . . . . aqueux

audacious . . . . audacieux

cancerous . . . . cancéreux

capricious . . . . capricieux

cavernous . . . . caverneux

ceremonious . . . . cérémonieux

conscientious . . . . consciencieux

contagious . . . . contagieux

copious . . . . copieux

courageous . . . . courageux

curious . . . . **curieux**

dangerous . . . . dangereux

delicious . . . . **délicieux**

    "This dinner is delicious.". . . . **« Ce dîner est délicieux. »**

desirous . . . . désireux

disastrous . . . . **désastreux**

dubious . . . . douteux

envious. . . . . envieux

fabulous . . . . fabuleux

facetious. . . . . facétieux

famous . . . . fameux *(more commonly "célèbre,"*
                              for people)

fastidious . . . . fastidieux *(meaning "boring,"*
                              "tiresome")

ferrous . . . . ferreux

fibrous . . . . fibreux

furious . . . . **furieux**

gaseous . . . . gazeux

gelatinous. . . . . gélatineux

generous . . . . **généreux**

    "My friend is generous." . . . . **« Mon ami est généreux. »**

glorious . . . . glorieux

gracious. . . . . gracieux *(meaning "graceful")*

harmonious. . . . . harmonieux

hideous . . . . hideux

ignominious . . . . ignominieux

imperious . . . . impérieux *(also used for "urgent")*

impetuous. . . . . impétueux

incestuous. . . . . incestueux

industrious . . . . industrieux *(more commonly "diligent")*

infectious . . . . infectieux

ingenious . . . . ingénieux

injurious . . . . injurieux

insidious . . . . insidieux
intravenous . . . . intraveineux

joyous . . . . joyeux
judicious . . . . judicieux

laborious . . . . laborieux
licentious . . . . licencieux
litigious . . . . litigieux
luminous . . . . lumineux
luxurious . . . . luxueux

marvelous . . . . merveilleux
melodious . . . . mélodieux
meticulous . . . . méticuleux
miraculous . . . . miraculeux
monstrous . . . . monstrueux
mountainous . . . . montagneux
mysterious . . . . **mystérieux**

nebulous . . . . nébuleux
nervous . . . . **nerveux**
numerous . . . . nombreux

oblivious . . . . oublieux
obsequious . . . . obséquieux
odious . . . . odieux
onerous . . . . onéreux *(meaning "costly,"*
"expensive")
outrageous . . . . outrageux *(more commonly*
"scandaleux")

perilous . . . . périlleux
pernicious . . . . pernicieux
pious . . . . pieux
piteous . . . . piteux

pompous . . . . pompeux

populous . . . . populeux

porous . . . . poreux

precious . . . . **précieux**

"This jewelry is precious." . . . **« Ce bijou est précieux. »**

prestigious . . . . **prestigieux**

pretentious . . . . prétentieux

prodigious . . . . prodigieux

religious . . . . **religieux**

"That man is religious." . . . . . **« Cet homme est religieux. »**

rigorous . . . . rigoureux

ruinous . . . . ruineux

scandalous . . . . **scandaleux**

scrupulous . . . . scrupuleux

seditious . . . . séditieux

sentencious . . . . sentencieux

serious . . . . sérieux

sinuous . . . . sinueux

spacious . . . . **spacieux**

"My apartment is spacious." . . . **« Mon appartement est spacieux. »**

specious . . . . spécieux

studious . . . . studieux

sumptuous . . . . somptueux

superstitious . . . . superstitieux

tortuous . . . . **tortueux**

tumultuous . . . . tumultueux

unctuous . . . . onctueux

ungracious . . . . disgracieux

vaporous . . . . vaporeux

venomous . . . . venimeux

vicious . . . . vicieux *(more commonly "méchant")* victorious . . . . victorieux

vigorous . . . . vigoureux

virtuous . . . . **vertueux**

viscous . . . . visqueux

voluptuous . . . . voluptueux

19A.

Reliez les paires de mots synonymes ou associés.

1. spacieux	fameux
2. ambitieux	appétissant
3. curieux	charitable
4. délicieux	déterminé
5. prestigieux	vaste
6. nerveux	émotionnel
7. généreux	inquisiteur

19B.

Ecoutez et lisez l'histoire. Répondez aux questions suivantes avec des phrases complètes.

Après la visite <u>désastreuse</u> à Toulouse, les deux voyageurs sont prêts pour une fin de semaine <u>ambitieuse</u> à Bordeaux. Marie sait que cet endroit est célèbre pour ses cannelés[1] <u>délicieux</u>, mais elle n'en sait pas beaucoup plus sur la ville. Philippe est aussi très <u>curieux</u> de connaître Bordeaux. Son ami lui a dit (told him) **qu'il y a un air <u>mystérieux</u> là-bas. A l'université de Bordeaux il y a un programme <u>prestigieux</u> de langues étrangères. Marie dit : « Quiconque étudie** (whoever studies) **à l'étranger doit être <u>ambitieux</u>. » Ils logent dans un hôtel très <u>spacieux</u> et ils y sont** (they find it) **très bien. Avant de partir pour Limoges, Marie dit : « J'aime beaucoup Bordeaux, mais ce n'est pas un endroit <u>mystérieux</u>, peut-être que ton ami est un type <u>nerveux</u> ! »**

[1] Individual bell-shaped cake/flan, specialty of Bordeaux

1. Comment a été la visite de Toulouse ?

2. Comment sont les cannelés de Bordeaux ?

3. Qu'est-ce que l'ami de Philippe a dit sur cette ville ?

4. Quel est le programme prestigieux à l'université de Bordeaux ?

5. Comment est leur hôtel ?

Chapter 20

Many English words ending in "–sion" have the same ending in French.

French words ending in "–sion" are usually feminine nouns. For example,

a session = *une session*

ENGLISH . . . . FRENCH

All words and phrases in bold are on **Track 20** *of the accompanying CD.*

adhesion . . . . adhésion *(also used for "membership")*
admission . . . . admission *(more commonly "entrée")*
aggression . . . . agression
allusion . . . . allusion
apprehension . . . . appréhension
ascension . . . . ascension
aversion . . . . aversion

circumcision . . . . circoncision
cohesion . . . . cohésion
collision . . . . **collision**
collusion . . . . collusion
commission . . . . commission
compassion . . . . compassion
comprehension . . . . **compréhension**
compression . . . . compression
compulsion . . . . compulsion
concession . . . . concession
conclusion . . . . **conclusion**
confession . . . . confession
confusion . . . . **confusion**
    "There's a lot of confusion." . . **« Il y a beaucoup de confusion. »**
contusion . . . . contusion

conversion . . . . conversion
convulsion . . . . convulsion
corrosion . . . . corrosion

decision . . . . **décision**
    "It's an important decision." . . . **« C'est une décision importante. »**
decompression . . . . décompression
depression . . . . dépression *(also used for "nervous*
                                                breakdown")
derision . . . . dérision
diffusion . . . . diffusion
digression . . . . digression
dimension . . . . **dimension**
discussion . . . . discussion *(also used for "argument")*
disillusion . . . . désillusion
dispersion . . . . dispersion
dissension . . . . dissension
dissuasion . . . . dissuasion
diversion . . . . diversion
division . . . . **division**

effusion . . . . effusion
elision . . . . élision
emission . . . . émission *(also used for "TV/radio show")*
erosion . . . . érosion
evasion . . . . évasion *(meaning "escape")*
exclusion . . . . exclusion
excursion . . . . excursion
expansion . . . . expansion
explosion . . . . **explosion**
expression . . . . **expression**
expulsion . . . . expulsion
extension . . . . extension
extroversion . . . . extraversion

fission . . . . fission

fusion . . . . fusion *(meaning "merger")*

hypertension . . . . hypertension

illusion . . . . illusion
immersion . . . . immersion
implosion . . . . implosion
imprecision . . . . imprécision
impression . . . . **impression**
  "He made a good impression." . . . **« Il a fait bonne impression. »**
impulsion . . . . impulsion
incision . . . . incision
inclusion . . . . inclusion
incomprehension . . . . incompréhension
incursion . . . . incursion
indecision . . . . indécision
infusion . . . . infusion *(also used for "herbal tea")*
intercession . . . . intercession
intermission . . . . intermission *(for shows/theater, use "entracte")*

introversion . . . . introversion
intrusion . . . . intrusion
invasion . . . . invasion
inversion . . . . inversion

lesion . . . . lésion

mission . . . . **mission**

obsession . . . . obsession
occasion . . . . occasion *(also used for "opportunity," and as an adjective, "secondhand")*
omission . . . . omission
oppression . . . . oppression

passion . . . . **passion**

"It's my passion." . . . . « **C'est ma passion.** »

pension . . . . pension *(also used for "small hotel")*

percussion . . . . percussion

permission . . . . permission

persuasion . . . . persuasion

perversion . . . . perversion

possession . . . . possession

precision. . . . . **précision**

pretension. . . . . prétention

prevision . . . . prévision *(meaning "forecast")*

procession . . . . procession

profession. . . . . **profession**

profusion . . . . profusion

progression. . . . . progression

propulsion . . . . propulsion

provision . . . . provision

recession . . . . récession

regression. . . . . régression

remission . . . . rémission

repercussion . . . . répercussion

repression. . . . . répression

repulsion . . . . répulsion

revision . . . . révision

secession . . . . sécession

session . . . . **session**

subdivision . . . . subdivision

submersion . . . . submersion

submission . . . . soumission

subversion . . . . subversion

succession . . . . succession *(also used for "inheritance")*

supervision . . . . supervision

suppression. . . . . suppression

suspension . . . . suspension

television . . . . **télévision**

tension . . . . tension

transfusion . . . . transfusion

transgression . . . . transgression

transmission . . . . transmission

version . . . . version

vision . . . . **vision**

20A.

Reliez les paires de mots synonymes ou associés.

1. mission	impact
2. confusion	objectif
3. collision	chaos
4. tension	bombe
5. télévision	exactitude
6. précision	film
7. explosion	anxiété

20B.

Ecoutez et lisez l'histoire. Répondez aux questions suivantes avec des phrases complètes.

Dès qu'ils arrivent à Limoges, Marie déclare : « Nous avons une <u>mission</u> claire ici à Limoges. Tu sais que la porcelaine est une de mes <u>passions</u>, pas vrai ? Je dois trouver une nouvelle assiette (plate) en porcelaine pour ma collection. » Philippe dit : « Très bien, mais peut-être que nous pouvons la trouver à Versailles ? » Marie insiste : « Non ! Ma <u>décision</u> finale est prise ! Je veux une assiette de Limoges. » Philippe a l'<u>impression</u> que Marie ne plaisante pas (isn't kidding around) et il s'applique à la « <u>mission</u> de l'assiette. » Après un déjeuner fabuleux sur la place ils partent en chasse (the hunt). Il y avait un peu de <u>confusion</u> avec toutes les rues et les impasses, mais finalement il y a une <u>conclusion</u> heureuse : Marie trouve son assiette.

INSTANT French Vocabulary Builder

1. Quelle est la mission de Marie ?

2. Pourquoi est-ce qu'elle veut cette chose ?

3. Que dit Marie de sa décision ?

4. Quelle impression Philippe a-t-il de Marie ?

5. Pourquoi est-ce qu'il y avait un peu de confusion ?

Chapter 21 — -sis/-se

English words ending in "–sis" generally correspond to "–se" in French.

French words ending in "–se" are usually feminine nouns. For example,

a crisis = *une crise*

ENGLISH . . . . FRENCH

*All words and phrases in bold are on **Track 21** of the accompanying CD.*

analysis . . . . **analyse**
antithesis . . . . antithèse

basis . . . . base
biogenesis . . . . biogenèse

catalysis . . . . catalyse
cirrhosis . . . . cirrhose
crisis . . . . **crise**
　　"The economy is in a crisis." . . . « **L'économie est en crise.** »

dialysis . . . . **dialyse**

electrolysis . . . . électrolyse
emphasis . . . . **emphase** (*only used for speech*)

genesis . . . . **genèse**

hydrolysis . . . . hydrolyse
hypnosis . . . . **hypnose**
hypothesis . . . . **hypothèse**
　　"The hypothesis is interesting." . . « **L'hypothèse est intéressante.** »

metamorphosis . . . . **métamorphose**

metastasis . . . . métastase

microanalysis . . . . microanalyse

mitosis . . . . mitose

mononucleosis . . . . mononucléose

mycosis . . . . mycose

narcosis . . . . narcose

neurosis . . . . névrose

osmosis . . . . osmose

osteoporosis . . . . ostéoporose

parenthesis . . . . parenthèse

photogenesis . . . . photogenése

photosynthesis . . . . photosynthèse

psychoanalysis . . . . psychanalyse

psychosis . . . . psychose

sclerosis . . . . sclérose

scoliosis . . . . scoliose

self-analysis . . . . auto-analyse

self-hypnosis . . . . auto-hypnose

synthesis . . . . synthèse

thesis . . . . **thèse**

   "I'm writing my thesis." . . . . . **« J'écris ma thèse. »**

tuberculosis . . . . tuberculose

21A.

Reliez les paires de mots synonymes ou associés.

1. métamorphose   pendule
2. analyse   changement
3. crise   sang
4. emphase   étude
5. hypothèse   présomption
6. dialyse   problème
7. hypnose   accentuation

21B.

Ecoutez et lisez l'histoire. Répondez aux questions suivantes avec des phrases complètes.

Destination : Tours ! Philippe et Marie connaissent déjà (already know) **Tours assez bien. Alors ils ne mettent pas vraiment l'accent sur la ballade touristique. Au lieu de ça** (instead)**, ils vont chercher un cousin de Philippe qui étudie à Tours. Il s'appelle Charles et étudie l'économie. Il écrit sa <u>thèse</u> sur la <u>crise</u> financière du tiers-monde** (of the Third World)**. Charles dit : « Malheureusement, je n'ai pas ma propre <u>hypothèse</u> sur la façon d'arrêter la <u>crise</u> et... sans cette <u>hypothèse</u>, je ne peux pas faire ma <u>thèse</u> ! » Charles demande à Philippe : « Est-ce que tu peux m'aider ? » Philippe répond : « On va voir.... »**

1. Pourquoi est-ce qu'ils ne mettent pas vraiment l'accent sur la ballade touristique à Tours ?

2. Qu'est-qu'ils font alors à Tours?

3. Sur quoi Charles écrit-il sa thèse ?

4. Charles a-t-il une bonne hypothèse pour sa thèse ?

5. Qu'est-ce que Charles demande à Philippe ?

Chapter 22

Many English words ending in "–tion" have the same ending in French.

French words ending in "–tion" are usually feminine nouns. For example,

a celebration = *une célébration*

ENGLISH . . . . FRENCH

All words and phrases in bold are on **Track 22** *of the accompanying CD.*

abbreviation . . . . abréviation
abdication . . . . abdication
aberration . . . . aberration
abjection . . . . abjection
abnegation . . . . abnégation
abolition . . . . abolition
abomination . . . . abomination
absolution . . . . absolution
absorption . . . . absorption
abstention . . . . abstention
abstraction . . . . abstraction
acceleration . . . . accélération
acclamation . . . . acclamation
accreditation . . . . accréditation
accommodation . . . . accommodation *(meaning "adjustment," or "arrangement," not "hotel accommodation")*
accumulation . . . . accumulation
accusation . . . . accusation
acquisition . . . . acquisition
action . . . . **action** *(also used for "stock share")*
activation . . . . activation
adaptation . . . . adaptation

addition . . . . addition *(also used for "bill," "check")*

administration . . . . administration

admiration . . . . admiration

adoption . . . . adoption

adoration . . . . adoration

adulation . . . . adulation

affection. . . . . affection

affiliation . . . . affiliation

affirmation . . . . affirmation

affliction. . . . . affliction

agglomeration. . . . . agglomération

aggravation . . . . aggravation *(meaning "worsening")*

agitation. . . . . agitation

alienation . . . . aliénation

alimentation . . . . alimentation

allegation . . . . allégation

alliteration . . . . allitération

allocation . . . . allocation

alteration . . . . altération

altercation . . . . altercation

ambition. . . . . **ambition**

"She has ambition." . . . . **« Elle a de l'ambition. »**

amelioration . . . . amélioration

amputation . . . . amputation

animation . . . . animation

annihilation. . . . . annihilation

annotation . . . . annotation

anticipation. . . . . anticipation

apparition . . . . apparition

application . . . . application *(for "application form," use "formulaire")*

appreciation . . . . appréciation *(also used for "evaluation," "judgment")*

approximation. . . . . approximation

articulation . . . . articulation

aspiration. . . . . aspiration

assertion. . . . . assertion

assimilation. . . . . assimilation

association . . . . association

attention. . . . . **attention** *(also used for "look out!")*

attenuation . . . . atténuation

attraction . . . . attraction

attribution. . . . . attribution

audition . . . . audition

augmentation . . . . augmentation

authorization. . . . . autorisation

automation . . . . automatisation

aviation . . . . aviation *(also used for "air force")*

bastion. . . . . bastion

benediction. . . . . bénédiction

capitalization . . . . capitalisation

capitulation. . . . . capitulation

castration . . . . castration

celebration . . . . **célébration** *(for "party," use "fête")*

   "The (religious) celebration   **« La célébration**

    is tomorrow." . . . . **a lieu demain. »**

centralization . . . . centralisation

certification. . . . . certification

cessation . . . . cessation

circulation. . . . . circulation *(also used for "traffic")*

circumspection . . . . circonspection

citation. . . . . citation *(also used for "quotation")*

civilization . . . . civilisation

classification . . . . classification

coagulation . . . . coagulation

coalition. . . . . coalition

cohabitation . . . . cohabitation

collaboration . . . . collaboration

collection . . . . **collection**

colonization . . . . colonisation

coloration . . . . coloration
combination . . . . combinaison
combustion . . . . combustion
commemoration. . . . . commémoration
commercialization . . . . commercialisation
commiseration. . . . . commisération
commotion . . . . commotion *(meaning "concussion")*
communication . . . . communication *(also used for*
                                                "phone call")
compensation . . . . compensation
competition. . . . . compétition
compilation. . . . . compilation
complication . . . . complication
composition . . . . composition
concentration . . . . concentration
conception . . . . conception
conciliation. . . . . conciliation
condemnation . . . . condamnation
condensation . . . . condensation
condition . . . . **condition**
confection. . . . . confection
confederation . . . . confédération
configuration. . . . . configuration
confirmation . . . . confirmation
confiscation . . . . confiscation
confrontation. . . . . confrontation
congestion . . . . congestion
congregation . . . . congrégation
conjugation. . . . . conjugaison
conjunction. . . . . conjonction
connotation. . . . . connotation
conscription . . . . conscription
consecration . . . . consécration
conservation . . . . conservation
consideration . . . . considération
consolation. . . . . consolation

INSTANT French Vocabulary Builder

consolidation . . . . consolidation
constellation . . . . constellation
consternation . . . . consternation
constipation . . . . constipation
constitution . . . . constitution
construction . . . . construction
consultation . . . . consultation
consumption . . . . consommation
contamination . . . . contamination
contemplation . . . . contemplation
continuation . . . . continuation
contraception . . . . contraception
contraction . . . . contraction
contradiction. . . . . contradiction
contribution. . . . . contribution
contrition . . . . contrition
convection . . . . convection
convention . . . . convention
conversation . . . . **conversation**
   "His conversation   **« Sa conversation**
   is fascinating." . . . . **est fascinante. »**
conviction. . . . . conviction
convocation . . . . convocation
cooperation . . . . coopération
coordination . . . . **coordination**
copulation . . . . copulation
corporation. . . . . corporation
correction . . . . correction
correlation . . . . corrélation
corruption. . . . . corruption
creation . . . . création
cremation . . . . crémation

damnation . . . . damnation
decapitation . . . . décapitation
deceleration . . . . décélération

deception . . . . déception *(meaning "disappointment")*

declaration . . . . déclaration

decomposition. . . . . décomposition

decoration . . . . décoration

deduction . . . . déduction

defection . . . . défection *(also used for "cancellation")*

definition . . . . **définition**

deflation. . . . . déflation *(only used in an economic context)*

deformation . . . . déformation

degradation . . . . dégradation

dehydration . . . . déshydratation

delegation . . . . délégation

deliberation . . . . délibération

demarcation . . . . démarcation

demolition . . . . démolition

demonstration . . . . démonstration

denomination . . . . dénomination

denunciation. . . . . dénonciation

deportation. . . . . déportation

deposition . . . . déposition

depreciation . . . . dépréciation

deprivation . . . . privation

derivation. . . . . dérivation

description . . . . description

designation. . . . . désignation

desolation. . . . . désolation

destabilization . . . . déstabilisation

destination . . . . destination

destitution. . . . . destitution *(meaning "dismissal")*

destruction . . . . **destruction**

detection . . . . détection

detention . . . . détention

deterioration . . . . détérioration

determination . . . . détermination

detonation . . . . détonation

INSTANT French Vocabulary Builder

devaluation. . . . . dévaluation
devastation. . . . . dévastation
deviation . . . . déviation
devotion. . . . . dévotion *(only used in a religious context)*

diction . . . . diction
differentiation . . . . différentiation
digestion . . . . digestion
dilution. . . . . dilution
direction. . . . . **direction**
discoloration. . . . . décoloration
discretion . . . . discrétion
discrimination . . . . discrimination
disinfection. . . . . désinfection
disintegration . . . . désintégration
disposition . . . . disposition
disqualification . . . . disqualification
dissection . . . . dissection
dissertation. . . . . dissertation
dissimulation. . . . . dissimulation
dissipation . . . . dissipation
dissociation . . . . dissociation
dissolution . . . . dissolution
distillation. . . . . distillation
distinction. . . . . distinction
distraction. . . . . distraction
distribution . . . . distribution
diversification . . . . diversification
documentation . . . . documentation
domination . . . . domination
dramatization . . . . dramatisation *(also used for "exaggeration")*

edification . . . . édification
edition . . . . **édition**
education . . . . éducation

ejaculation	éjaculation
ejection	éjection
elaboration	élaboration
election	élection
electrocution	électrocution
elevation	élévation
elimination	élimination
elocution	élocution
elongation	élongation
elucidation	élucidation
emanation	émanation
emancipation	émancipation
emigration	émigration
emotion	**émotion**
emulation	émulation
enumeration	énumération
enunciation	énonciation
equation	équation
eradication	éradication
erection	érection
erudition	érudition
eruption	éruption
estimation	estimation
evacuation	évacuation
evaluation	évaluation
evaporation	évaporation
eviction	éviction
evocation	évocation
evolution	évolution
exaggeration	**exagération**

"That's an exaggeration." . . . **« C'est une exagération. »**

exasperation	exaspération
excavation	excavation
exception	exception
exclamation	exclamation
excretion	excrétion

execution . . . . exécution

exemption. . . . . exemption

exhibition . . . . exposition

exhortation . . . . exhortation

exoneration . . . . exonération

expedition . . . . expédition *(also used for "sending," "shipping")*

experimentation. . . . . expérimentation

expiration. . . . . expiration

explanation. . . . . explication

exploitation. . . . . exploitation

exploration . . . . exploration

exportation . . . . exportation

exposition. . . . . exposition

extermination . . . . extermination

extinction . . . . extinction

extraction . . . . extraction

extradition . . . . extradition

exultation . . . . exultation

fabrication . . . . fabrication *(meaning "manufacturing")*

faction . . . . faction

falsification . . . . falsification

fascination . . . . fascination

federation. . . . . fédération *(meaning "league")*

fermentation . . . . fermentation

fertilization . . . . fertilisation

fiction. . . . . fiction

filtration . . . . filtration

fixation. . . . . fixation

flagellation . . . . flagellation

fluctuation. . . . . fluctuation

formation . . . . formation *(also used for "training")*

formulation . . . . formulation

fornication . . . . fornication

fortification . . . . fortification

foundation	**fondation**
fraction	fraction
friction	friction
frustration	frustration
fumigation	fumigation
function	fonction
generalization	généralisation
generation	**génération**
germination	germination
gestation	gestation
globalization	globalisation
glorification	glorification
gradation	gradation
gravitation	gravitation
habitation	habitation
hallucination	hallucination
hesitation	hésitation
hibernation	hibernation
humiliation	humiliation
identification	identification
illumination	illumination
illustration	illustration
imagination	imagination
imitation	**imitation**

"This painting is an imitation." . . **« Ce tableau est une imitation. »**

immigration	immigration
immunization	immunisation
imperfection	imperfection
implication	implication
importation	importation
imposition	imposition
impregnation	imprégnation
improvisation	improvisation

inaction . . . . inaction

inauguration . . . . inauguration

incarceration. . . . . incarcération

incarnation . . . . incarnation

incineration. . . . . incinération

inclination. . . . . inclination

incrimination . . . . incrimination

incubation . . . . incubation

indetermination . . . . indétermination

indication . . . . indication

indignation . . . . indignation

indiscretion . . . . indiscrétion *(meaning "nosiness,"*
"inquisitiveness")

infatuation . . . . infatuation *(meaning "vanity")*

infection . . . . infection *(also used for "stench,"*
"vile smell")

infiltration . . . . infiltration

inflammation . . . . inflammation

inflation . . . . inflation

information . . . . **information**

inhibition . . . . inhibition

initiation. . . . . initiation

injection . . . . injection

Inquisition. . . . . Inquisition

innovation . . . . innovation

inscription. . . . . inscription *(also used for "registration")*

insemination . . . . insémination

insertion . . . . insertion

inspection . . . . inspection

inspiration . . . . inspiration *(also used for "breath,"*
"inhalation")

installation . . . . installation

institution . . . . institution

instruction. . . . . instruction

insurrection . . . . insurrection

integration . . . . intégration

intensification . . . . intensification
intention . . . . **intention**
interaction . . . . interaction
interception. . . . . interception
interrogation . . . . interrogation
interruption . . . . interruption
interpretation . . . . interprétation
intersection . . . . intersection
intervention. . . . . intervention *(also used for "surgery,"*
"operation")
intimidation. . . . . intimidation
intonation . . . . intonation
intoxication. . . . . intoxication *(meaning "poisoning")*
introduction. . . . . introduction
introspection . . . . introspection
intuition . . . . intuition
inundation . . . . inondation
invention . . . . **invention**
investigation . . . . investigation
invitation . . . . invitation
irradiation . . . . irradiation
irrigation . . . . irrigation
irritation . . . . irritation
isolation . . . . isolation *(also used for "insulation")*

jubilation . . . . jubilation
jurisdiction . . . . juridiction
justification . . . . justification
juxtaposition . . . . juxtaposition

laceration. . . . . lacération
lamentation. . . . . lamentation
legalization. . . . . légalisation
legislation. . . . . législation
levitation . . . . lévitation
liberation . . . . libération

limitation . . . . limitation
liquidation . . . . liquidation
locomotion . . . . locomotion
lotion . . . . **lotion**
lubrication . . . . lubrification

machination . . . . machination
malediction. . . . . malédiction
malformation. . . . . malformation
malnutrition. . . . . malnutrition
manifestation . . . . manifestation *(also used for "public demonstration")*

manipulation. . . . . manipulation
masturbation. . . . . masturbation
maturation . . . . maturation
maximization . . . . maximalisation
mechanization . . . . mécanisation
mediation . . . . médiation
meditation . . . . méditation
mention . . . . mention *(noun only)*
migration . . . . migration
mobilization . . . . mobilisation
moderation . . . . modération
modification . . . . modification
modulation . . . . modulation
monopolization . . . . monopolisation
mortification . . . . mortification
motion . . . . motion *(only used for "proposal")*
motivation. . . . . motivation
multiplication . . . . multiplication
mutation. . . . . mutation
mutilation . . . . mutilation
mystification . . . . mystification

narration . . . . narration
nation . . . . **nation**

navigation . . . . navigation
negation. . . . . négation
negotiation . . . . négociation
nomination . . . . nomination
notation . . . . notation
notion . . . . notion
nutrition . . . . nutrition

objection . . . . objection
obligation. . . . . obligation
obliteration . . . . oblitération
observation. . . . . observation
obstruction . . . . obstruction
occupation . . . . occupation
operation . . . . **opération**
opposition . . . . opposition
option . . . . option
organization. . . . . organisation
orientation . . . . orientation
oxidation . . . . oxydation

pagination . . . . pagination
palpitation . . . . palpitation
participation . . . . participation
partition . . . . partition *(also used for "music score")*
penetration . . . . pénétration
perception . . . . perception
perdition. . . . . perdition
perfection . . . . perfection
perforation . . . . perforation
permutation . . . . permutation
perpetuation . . . . perpétuation
persecution . . . . persécution
personification . . . . personnification
perspiration . . . . transpiration
petition. . . . . pétition

pigmentation. . . . . pigmentation

plantation . . . . plantation

pollution . . . . pollution

popularization. . . . . popularisation

population . . . . **population**

portion . . . . portion

position . . . . **position** *(for employment, use "situation")*

potion . . . . potion

precaution . . . . précaution

precipitation . . . . précipitation

predestination . . . . prédestination

prediction. . . . . prédiction

predilection. . . . . prédilection

predisposition . . . . prédisposition

premeditation . . . . préméditation

premonition . . . . prémonition

preoccupation . . . . **préoccupation**

   "It's a constant   **« C'est une préoccupation**

   preoccupation." . . . . **constante. »**

preparation. . . . . préparation

preposition . . . . préposition

presentation . . . . présentation

preservation . . . . préservation

presumption . . . . présomption

pretension. . . . . prétention

prevention . . . . prévention

privation. . . . . privation

privatization . . . . privatisation

probation . . . . probation

proclamation. . . . . proclamation

procreation. . . . . procréation

production . . . . production

prohibition . . . . prohibition

projection . . . . projection

proliferation . . . . prolifération

prolongation . . . . prolongation

promotion . . . . promotion

pronunciation . . . . prononciation

proportion . . . . proportion

proposition . . . . proposition

prostitution . . . . prostitution

prostration . . . . prostration

protection . . . . protection

provocation . . . . provocation

publication . . . . publication

punctuation . . . . ponctuation

purification . . . . purification

putrefaction . . . . putréfaction

qualification . . . . qualification

question . . . . question

radiation . . . . radiation

ramification . . . . ramification

ratification . . . . ratification

ration . . . . ration

reaction . . . . **réaction**

   "Your reaction is ridiculous." . . **« Ta réaction est ridicule. »**

realization . . . . réalisation *(meaning "completion")*

reception . . . . réception

recitation . . . . récitation

recommendation . . . . recommandation

reconciliation . . . . réconciliation

recreation . . . . récréation

recrimination . . . . récrimination

recuperation . . . . récupération

redemption . . . . rédemption

reduction . . . . réduction

reelection . . . . réélection

refraction . . . . réfraction

refrigeration . . . . réfrigération

reflection . . . . réflexion

regeneration . . . . régénération

regulation. . . . . régulation

rehabilitation. . . . . réhabilitation

reincarnation . . . . réincarnation

relation . . . . relation

relegation. . . . . relégation

remuneration. . . . . rémunération

renovation . . . . rénovation

renunciation . . . . renonciation

reorganization . . . . réorganisation

reparation . . . . réparation

repetition . . . . répétition

replication . . . . réplication

representation . . . . représentation

reproduction . . . . reproduction

reputation. . . . . **réputation**

　　"He has a bad reputation." . . **« Il a une mauvaise réputation. »**

requisition. . . . . réquisition

reservation . . . . réservation

resignation . . . . résignation *(only used for feelings; "job resignation" is "démission")*

resolution . . . . résolution

respiration . . . . respiration

restitution . . . . restitution

restoration . . . . restauration

restriction . . . . restriction

resurrection. . . . . résurrection

retention. . . . . rétention

retraction . . . . rétractation

retribution. . . . . rétribution

revelation . . . . révélation

reverberation . . . . réverbération

revocation . . . . révocation

revolution . . . . **révolution**

    "There was a revolution.". . . . **« Il y a eu une révolution. »**

rotation . . . . rotation

salutation . . . . salutation

sanction . . . . sanction

satisfaction . . . . **satisfaction**

saturation . . . . saturation

secretion. . . . . sécrétion

section . . . . section

sedation . . . . sédation

sedition . . . . sédition

seduction . . . . séduction

sedimentation . . . . sédimentation

segmentation . . . . segmentation

segregation . . . . ségrégation

selection. . . . . sélection

self-destruction. . . . . autodestruction

sensation . . . . sensation

separation . . . . séparation

simplification. . . . . simplification

simulation. . . . . simulation

situation . . . . **situation** *(also used for "job position")*

    "The situation is difficult.". . . . **« La situation est difficile. »**

solution . . . . **solution**

    "I don't see a solution." . . . . . **« Je ne vois pas de solution. »**

specialization . . . . spécialisation

specification . . . . spécification

speculation . . . . spéculation

stabilization . . . . stabilisation

stagnation . . . . stagnation

station . . . . **station** *(only used for "bus station";*
                                         "train station" is "gare")

    "The bus station is close." . . . **« La station de bus est proche. »**

sterilization. . . . . stérilisation

stimulation . . . . stimulation

stipulation . . . . stipulation
strangulation . . . . strangulation
subordination . . . . subordination
substitution . . . . substitution
subtraction . . . . soustraction
suffocation . . . . suffocation
suggestion . . . . suggestion
superstition . . . . superstition
supposition . . . . supposition
synchronization . . . . synchronisation

taxation . . . . taxation *(more commonly "imposition")*
telecommunication . . . . télécommunication
temptation . . . . tentation
traction. . . . . traction
tradition . . . . **tradition**
  "It's a tradition." . . . . **« C'est une tradition. »**
transaction . . . . transaction
transcription . . . . transcription
transformation . . . . transformation
transition . . . . transition
translation. . . . . traduction
trepidation . . . . trépidation
tribulation . . . . tribulations *(only used in the plural)*

unification . . . . unification
urbanization . . . . urbanisation
utilization . . . . utilisation

vaccination . . . . vaccination
validation . . . . validation
variation. . . . . variation
vegetation . . . . végétation
veneration . . . . vénération
ventilation. . . . . ventilation
verification . . . . vérification

vibration. . . . . vibration
violation . . . . violation
vocation . . . . vocation
vocalization . . . . vocalisation

INSTANT French Vocabulary Builder

22A.

Reliez les paires de mots synonymes ou associés.

1. station		circonstance
2. situation		route
3. réaction		donation
4. direction		bus
5. célébration		anniversaire
6. contribution		pays
7. nation		réponse

22B.

Ecoutez et lisez l'histoire. Répondez aux questions suivantes avec des phrases complètes.

Dans la <u>station</u> de bus d'Orléans, Philippe et Marie voient une affiche (a sign) **pour une grande <u>célébration</u> sur la place principale ce soir. Ils lisent l'<u>information</u> et comprennent que ce sera une grande fête. Marie ne veut pas y aller parce qu'elle ne se sent pas bien** (she doesn't feel well)**. Philippe dit : « À ton tour de me faire une faveur. » Marie voit que la <u>réaction</u> de Philippe est forte et elle dit : « Très bien, allons-y. » Philippe dit : « Quelle grande <u>célébration</u> ! Ce sont des <u>conditions</u> parfaites pour découvrir cette belle ville et sa cuisine. » La <u>réaction</u> de Marie est plus sobre** (subdued)**. Elle dit : « Oui, nous avons une bonne <u>position</u> ici. » A la fin de la fête, Philippe est plus calme. Il dit : « Marie, j'ai trop mangé et trop bu, je dois aller dormir. »**

1. Où voient-ils l'affiche pour la célébration ?

2. Comment sera cette fête ?

3. Pourquoi est-ce que la célébration est intéressante pour Philippe ?

4. Comment est la réaction de Marie ?

5. À la fin de la fête comment se sent Philippe ?

-ty/-té

English words ending in "–ty" generally correspond to "–té" in French.

French words ending in "–té" are usually feminine nouns. For example,

an activity = *une activité*

ENGLISH . . . . FRENCH

All words and phrases in bold are on **Track 23** *of the accompanying CD.*

abnormality . . . . anormalité
absurdity . . . . absurdité
accessibility . . . . accessibilité
acidity . . . . acidité
activity . . . . **activité**
actuality . . . . actualité *(also used for "news," "current events")*
adversity . . . . adversité
affinity . . . . affinité
agility . . . . agilité
ambiguity . . . . ambiguïté
amenity . . . . aménité *(meaning "pleasantness")*
amorality . . . . amoralité
animosity . . . . animosité
antiquity . . . . antiquité *(also used for "antiques")*
anxiety . . . . **anxiété**
atrocity . . . . atrocité
austerity . . . . austérité
authenticity . . . . authenticité
authority . . . . autorité
avidity . . . . avidité

banality . . . . banalité

beauty . . . . beauté

bestiality . . . . bestialité

brevity . . . . brièveté

brutality . . . . brutalité

calamity . . . . calamité

capacity . . . . capacité

captivity . . . . captivité

cavity . . . . cavité *(for teeth, use "carrie")*

celebrity . . . . **célébrité**

charity . . . . charité

chastity . . . . chasteté

city . . . . cité *(only used for "historic center"*
of a city)

civility . . . . civilité

clarity . . . . clarté

commodity . . . . commodité *(meaning "convenience,"*
"comfort")

community . . . . **communauté** *(only used in a cultural*
or religious context)

compatibility . . . . compatibilité

complexity . . . . complexité

complicity . . . . complicité

confidentiality . . . . confidentialité

conformity . . . . conformité

continuity . . . . continuité

cordiality . . . . cordialité

creativity . . . . **créativité**

"He has a lot of creativity." . . **« Il a beaucoup de créativité. »**

credibility . . . . crédibilité

credulity . . . . crédulité

cruelty . . . . cruauté

culpability . . . . culpabilité

curiosity . . . . **curiosité**

debility . . . . débilité

deformity . . . . difformité

density . . . . densité

deputy . . . . député *(meaning*
"elected official")

dexterity . . . . dextérité

difficulty . . . . **difficulté**

dignity . . . . dignité

disparity . . . . disparité

diversity . . . . diversité

divinity . . . . divinité

duality . . . . dualité

duplicity . . . . duplicité

durability . . . . durabilité

eccentricity . . . . excentricité

elasticity . . . . élasticité

electricity . . . . **électricité**

enormity . . . . énormité

entity . . . . entité

equality . . . . égalité

equity . . . . équité

eternity . . . . éternité

eventuality . . . . éventualité

extremity . . . . extrémité

facility . . . . facilité *(meaning "ease" or "ability")*

faculty . . . . faculté *(meaning "ability" and*
"university department")

falsity . . . . fausseté

familiarity . . . . familiarité

fatality . . . . fatalité *(meaning "fate")*

feasibility . . . . faisabilité

felicity . . . . félicité

femininity . . . . féminité

ferocity . . . . férocité

fertility . . . . fertilité

fidelity	fidélité
flexibility	**flexibilité**
"His flexibility is	**« Sa flexibilité est**
exceptional."	**exceptionnelle. »**
fluidity	fluidité
formality	formalité
fragility	fragilité
fraternity	fraternité
frugality	frugalité
futility	futilité
gaiety	gaieté
generality	généralité
generosity	**générosité**
gratuity	gratuité *(meaning "free," "no cost")*
gravity	gravité
heredity	hérédité
hilarity	hilarité
heterosexuality	hétérosexualité
homosexuality	homosexualité
honesty	honnêteté
hospitality	hospitalité
hostility	hostilité
humanity	humanité
humidity	humidité
humility	humilité
identity	**identité**
"Here is my ID (identity) card." . .	**« Voici ma carte d'identité. »**
illegality	illégalité
immaturity	immaturité
immensity	immensité
immobility	immobilité
immorality	immoralité
immortality	immortalité

immunity. . . . . immunité

impartiality . . . . impartialité

impetuosity . . . . impétuosité

impiety. . . . . impiété

impossibility . . . . **impossibilité**

improbability . . . . improbabilité

impunity. . . . . impunité

impurity . . . . impureté

inactivity. . . . . inactivité

incapacity. . . . . incapacité

incompatibility. . . . . incompatibilité

incongruity . . . . incongruité

incredulity. . . . . incrédulité

indemnity . . . . indemnité

indignity. . . . . indignité

individuality . . . . individualité

indivisibility. . . . . indivisibilité

inequality . . . . inégalité

infallibility. . . . . infaillibilité

inferiority . . . . infériorité

infertility. . . . . infertilité

infidelity . . . . infidélité

infinity . . . . infinité *(more commonly "infini")*

infirmity . . . . infirmité

inflammability . . . . inflammabilité

inflexibility . . . . inflexibilité

ingenuity . . . . ingéniosité

inhumanity . . . . inhumanité

iniquity. . . . . iniquité

insatiability . . . . insatiabilité

insensibility . . . . insensibilité

insensitivity . . . . insensibilité

instability . . . . instabilité

integrity . . . . intégrité

intensity . . . . **intensité**

invincibility . . . . invincibilité

invisibility . . . . invisibilité
irregularity . . . . irrégularité
irresponsibility. . . . . irresponsabilité

legality. . . . . légalité
liberty . . . . **liberté**
    "I visited the Statue   **« J'ai visité la statue de**
      of Liberty." . . . . **la Liberté. »**
liquidity . . . . liquidité
longevity . . . . longévité
loyalty . . . . loyauté
lucidity. . . . . lucidité *(more commonly "clarté")*

magnanimity. . . . . magnanimité
majesty . . . . majesté
majority . . . . majorité *(also used for "adulthood")*
masculinity . . . . masculinité
maternity . . . . maternité
maturity . . . . maturité
mediocrity . . . . médiocrité
mentality. . . . . mentalité
minority . . . . minorité *(also used for "under 18*
                                   years old")
mobility . . . . mobilité
modernity. . . . . modernité
monstrosity . . . . monstruosité
morality . . . . moralité
mortality. . . . . mortalité
multiplicity . . . . multiplicité
municipality . . . . municipalité

nationality . . . . nationalité
nativity. . . . . nativité
necessity. . . . . **nécessité**
neutrality . . . . neutralité
normality . . . . normalité

notoriety	notoriété
novelty	nouveauté
nudity	nudité
obesity	obésité
objectivity	objectivité
obscenity	obscénité
obscurity	obscurité
opportunity	**opportunité** *(more commonly "occasion")*
originality	originalité
parity	parité
partiality	partialité
particularity	particularité
passivity	passivité
paternity	paternité
peculiarity	particularité
penalty	pénalité
perpetuity	perpétuité
perplexity	perplexité
personality	**personnalité**
"He has a charming personality."	**« Il a une charmante personnalité. »**
perversity	perversité
piety	piété
placidity	placidité
plasticity	plasticité
plausibility	plausibilité
plurality	pluralité
polarity	polarité
popularity	popularité
possibility	**possibilité**
posterity	postérité
poverty	pauvreté
principality	principauté

priority	priorité
probability	probabilité
productivity	productivité
promiscuity	promiscuité
property	propriété
prosperity	prospérité
proximity	proximité
puberty	puberté
publicity	publicité *(also used for "advertising")*
punctuality	ponctualité
purity	pureté

quality	**qualité**
quantity	**quantité**

rapidity	rapidité
rarity	rareté
rationality	rationalité
reality	réalité
reciprocity	réciprocité
regularity	régularité
relativity	relativité
respectability	respectabilité
responsibility	**responsabilité**
"I have a lot of responsibilities."	**« J'ai beaucoup de responsabilités. »**
rigidity	rigidité
royalty	royauté

sanctity	sainteté
satiety	satiété
security	sécurité
senility	sénilité
sensibility	sensibilité *(also used for "sensitivity")*
sensuality	sensualité
sentimentality	sentimentalité

serenity . . . . sérénité
severity. . . . . sévérité
sexuality. . . . . sexualité
similarity. . . . . similarité
simplicity . . . . simplicité
sincerity . . . . sincérité
singularity. . . . . singularité
sobriety . . . . sobriété
society . . . . société
solemnity . . . . solennité
solidarity . . . . solidarité
solidity. . . . . solidité
solubility. . . . . solubilité
speciality . . . . **spécialité**
specificity . . . . spécificité
spirituality. . . . . spiritualité
spontaneity . . . . spontanéité
stability . . . . stabilité
sterility . . . . stérilité
stupidity . . . . stupidité
subjectivity . . . . subjectivité
subtlety. . . . . subtilité
superiority . . . . supériorité
surety. . . . . sûreté *(also used for "safety," "sureness")*

tangibility . . . . tangibilité
technicality . . . . technicité
tenacity . . . . ténacité
timidity. . . . . timidité
tonality. . . . . tonalité
totality . . . . totalité
tranquility . . . . tranquillité
treaty . . . . traité *(also used for "treatise")*
trinity . . . . trinité
triviality . . . . trivialité *(also used for "vulgarity")*

ubiquity . . . . ubiquité

unanimity . . . . unanimité

uniformity . . . . uniformité

unity . . . . unité

university . . . . **université**

    "You are going to   **« Tu vas à**

    the university." . . . . **l'université. »**

utility . . . . utilité *(meaning "usefulness")*

validity . . . . validité

vanity . . . . vanité

variety . . . . variété

velocity . . . . vélocité

veracity . . . . véracité

verity . . . . vérité *(meaning "truth")*

versatility . . . . versatilité *(meaning "fickleness")*

viability . . . . viabilité

virginity . . . . virginité

virility . . . . virilité

virtuosity . . . . virtuosité

viscosity . . . . viscosité

visibility . . . . **visibilité**

vitality . . . . vitalité

vivacity . . . . vivacité

volatility . . . . volatilité

voracity . . . . voracité

vulgarity . . . . vulgarité

vulnerability . . . . vulnérabilité

23A.

Reliez les paires de mots synonymes ou associés.

1. université	chance
2. difficulté	abondance
3. impossibilité	imagination
4. activité	mouvement
5. opportunité	professeur
6. créativité	infaisabilité
7. quantité	obstacle

23B.

Ecoutez et lisez l'histoire. Répondez aux questions suivantes avec des phrases complètes.

La dernière ville (last city) **pour Philippe et Marie, c'est Versailles. Marie est très enthousiaste ; elle dit que Versailles est une ville où il y a beaucoup de <u>créativité</u>, d'<u>originalité</u> et d'<u>activité</u>. Philippe dit qu'il aime beaucoup la <u>personnalité</u> de cet endroit. Versailles est une belle ville et ils y restent quatre jours. Un jour Marie croit voir** (she thinks she sees) **une <u>célébrité</u> : Jean Reno. Mais Philippe dit que c'est impossible, parce que Jean Reno tourne un film en Suisse. Avant de rentrer à la maison** (before going home)**, Philippe dit : « Écoute Marie, j'ai une question, est-ce que nous pourrions vivre ici, à Versailles, un jour ? » Marie répond : « Oui, oui, il y a beaucoup de <u>possibilités</u> pour nous ici. On va voir…. »**

1. Que dit Marie de Versailles ?

2. Qu'est-ce que Philippe aime dans cette ville ?

3. Combien de jours restent-ils à Versailles?

4. Est-ce que Marie voit une célébrité ?

5. Est-ce que Marie veut vivre à Versailles un jour ? Qu'est-ce qu'elle dit ?

ANSWER KEY

1A.

1. animal: zoo
2. total: complet
3. social: convivial
4. original: unique
5. légal: permis
6. crucial: essentiel
7. principal: capital

1B.

1. Ils sont de Strasbourg.
2. Il veut faire un voyage international.
3. Elle veut faire un voyage national.
4. Il dit que l'idée de Marie n'est pas originale.
5. Selon Philippe, l'oncle de Marie est trop antisocial et traditionnel.

2A.

1. distance: loin
2. ambulance: hôpital
3. tolérance: respect
4. arrogance: vanité
5. importance: proéminence
6. persévérance: détermination
7. fragrance: parfum

2B.

1. Il parle de l'importance de ne pas dépenser beaucoup.
2. Oui, il y a beaucoup de distance à parcourir.
3. Il faudra de la persévérance.
4. Oui, elle comprend l'importance de ne pas dépenser beaucoup d'argent.
5. Il répond : « On va voir…. »

3A.

1. restaurant: dîner
2. important: essentiel
3. élégant: chic
4. abondant: copieux
5. arrogant: vanité
6. immigrant: étranger
7. éléphant: animal

3B.

1. Ils vont à Paris.
2. Elle pense qu'ils sont arrogants.
3. Il dit que leur façon de s'habiller est élégante.
4. Il dit que l'histoire de Paris est très importante.
5. Le restaurant s'appelle L'éléphant rouge.

4A.

1. spectaculaire: sensationnel
2. polaire: froid
3. solaire: soleil
4. circulaire: sphérique
5. nucléaire: atomique
6. vulgaire: indécent
7. cardio-vasculaire: cœur

4B.

1. Ils font une promenade.
2. Il utilise un téléphone portable.
3. Son italien est spectaculaire.
4. Il étudie la physique nucléaire.
5. Les conversations de son ami sont plutôt circulaires.

5A.

1. nécessaire: obligatoire

2. ordinaire: commun

3. contraire: opposé

4. anniversaire: célébration

5. dictionnaire: définition

6. salaire: argent

7. secrétaire: assistant

5B.

1. L'itinéraire de Philippe et Marie à Paris est très compliqué.

2. Elle filme un documentaire.

3. Il dit que le rythme est extraordinaire.

4. Selon Philippe, il n'est pas nécessaire de filmer chaque détail.

5. Elle répond : « Au contraire, c'est très important de filmer chaque détail ! »

6A.

1. visible: perceptible

2. incroyable: extraordinaire

3. horrible: très mal

4. inflexible: rigide

5. comparable: similaire

6. probable: possible

7. adorable: mignon

6B.

1. Après Paris, ils vont en Corse.

2. Elle pense que Philippe est très irresponsable.

3. Il dit que Marie est inflexible.

4. Non, elle pense que c'est assez improbable.

5. Elle demande s'il sera possible d'acheter les billets pour le spectacle de danse en Corse.

7A.

1. respect: admiration
2. direct: immédiat
3. correct: exact
4. contact: adresse
5. aspect: partie
6. exact: précis
7. incorrect: erroné

7B.

1. Ils ont pris un vol direct.
2. Elle pense que ce n'est pas la destination correcte parce qu'elle ne comprend pas tout.
3. Elle ne comprend pas le français en Corse parce qu'ils parlent un dialecte.
4. Le contact de Philippe s'appelle Alphonse.
5. Il a beaucoup de respect pour Philippe et sa petite amie Marie.

8A.

1. patience: calme
2. différence: distinction
3. innocence: naïveté
4. violence: guerre
5. science: biologie
6. conférence: réunion
7. expérience: maturité

8B.

1. Il dit : « Quelle coïncidence ! Ma petite amie et moi allons à la danse demain soir. »
2. Selon Marie, la persistance et la patience aident.
3. Il pense que ce sera une bonne expérience.
4. Il ressent de l'indifférence.
5. Il est désolé de son impatience.

9A.

1. président: directeur
2. urgent: pressant
3. continent: Europe
4. client: consommateur
5. patient: calme
6. intelligent: intellectuel
7. différent: distinct

9B.

1. Elle reçoit un message urgent.
2. Il est directeur d'un établissement médical.
3. Elle dit que son cousin est différent/compétent/intelligent/étrange.
4. Oui, selon Marie il est très, très intelligent.
5. Il dit : « Bon, on va voir…. »

10A.

1. allergie: pollen
2. stratégie: tactique
3. psychologie: mental
4. géologie: pierre
5. énergie: dynamisme
6. chronologie: temps
7. trilogie: trois

10B.

1. Il a beaucoup d'énergie.
2. Non, le café ne donne pas d'allergies aux jeunes.
3. Il parle de ses nouvelles technologies médicales.
4. Non, il n'étudie pas la radiologie.
5. Non, elle n'étudie pas la psychologie.

11A.

1. stratégique: tactique
2. électronique: radio
3. artistique: créatif
4. classique: romain
5. ironique: sarcastique
6. authentique: véritable
7. historique: date

11B.

1. Ils visitent des musées artistiques.
2. Nice est magique le soir.
3. Nice est une ville fantastique.
4. Quand il conduit, il y a beaucoup de circulation.
5. Selon Marie, ce n'est pas très romantique de passer les vacances en voiture.

12A.

1. typique: normal
2. botanique: jardin
3. pratique: rationnel
4. électrique: lampe
5. éthique: moralité
6. biologique: humain
7. magique: mystique

12B.

1. Il veut rester à Nice.
2. Elle veut voyager d'une façon logique.
3. Oui, elle a le sens pratique.
4. Ils vont à Marseille.
5. Elle dit : « Toi aussi tu veux aller à Marseille, pas vrai ? »

13A.

1. valide: vrai
2. rigide: inflexible
3. acide: citron
4. liquide: fluide
5. timide: réservé
6. stupide: idiot
7. splendide: magnifique

13B.

1. Elle dit que c'est un plan stupide.
2. Il pense que c'est une idée splendide.
3. Pendant le voyage il fait très humide.
4. Il dit qu'il doit boire beaucoup de liquide.
5. Il dit qu'il ne doit pas manger de nourriture acide.

14A.

1. communisme: Karl Marx
2. optimisme: positif
3. impressionisme: art
4. féminisme: femme
5. nationalisme: patriotisme
6. tourisme: passeport
7. terrorisme: bombe

14B.

1. Oui, il y a beaucoup de tourisme à Marseille.
2. Le livre parle de l'influence du socialisme, du fascisme et du communisme en France.
3. Le livre décrit le nationalisme français.
4. Elle demande à Philippe ce qu'il pense du capitalisme.
5. Il dit : « Mangeons une glace ! »

15A.

1. artiste: peintre
2. touriste: visiteur
3. pessimiste: négatif
4. optimiste: positif
5. dentiste: dent
6. finaliste: compétition
7. fleuriste: bouquet

15B.

1. Il est dentiste.
2. Oui, ce sont des touristes « professionnels. »
3. Elle a une liste de questions.
4. Le dentiste est pessimiste et réaliste.
5. L'artiste est optimiste et idéaliste.

16A.

1. consécutif: successif
2. créatif: artistique
3. positif: optimiste
4. exécutif: patron
5. motif: cause
6. négatif: fataliste
7. objectif: impartial

16B.

1. Il avait entendu des choses négatives.
2. Il pense que c'est une région créative et compétitive.
3. Elle a une impression positive.
4. Juvignac est un village pas très actif mais très accueillant.
5. Ils passent deux jours consécutifs là-bas.

17A.

1. docteur: médecin
2. acteur: théâtre
3. sénateur: congrès
4. professeur: université
5. inventeur: innovateur
6. moteur: voiture
7. terreur: peur

17B.

1. Elle remarque de la terreur.
2. Il dit : « Quelle erreur de venir ici ! »
3. Il dit : « Fais-moi une faveur : dis-moi que je n'ai pas besoin d'aller à cette fête. »
4. Non, l'acteur n'est pas célèbre.
5. Non, le sénateur est vieux.

18A.

1. territoire: zone
2. accessoire: ceinture
3. contradictoire: paradoxal
4. laboratoire: recherche
5. obligatoire: nécessaire
6. ivoire: éléphant
7. victoire: gagner

18B.

1. Il vont à Bordeaux.
2. Il aurait préféré une auberge.
3. Il dit que la fête était pire que le purgatoire.
4. Non, ce n'est pas vrai. Sa présence était obligatoire.
5. Non, il ne répond pas au dernier commentaire contradictoire de Marie.

19A.

1. spacieux: vaste
2. ambitieux: déterminé
3. curieux: inquisiteur
4. délicieux: appétissant
5. prestigieux: fameux
6. nerveux: émotionnel
7. généreux: charitable

19B.

1. La visite de Toulouse a été désastreuse.
2. Ils sont délicieux.
3. Il a dit qu'il y a un air mystérieux là-bas.
4. Le programme prestigieux est le programme de langues étrangères.
5. Leur hôtel est très spacieux.

20A.

1. mission: objectif
2. confusion: chaos
3. collision: impact
4. tension: anxiété
5. télévision: film
6. précision: exactitude
7. explosion: bombe

20B.

1. Sa mission est de trouver une nouvelle assiette en porcelaine.
2. Elle veut cette chose pour sa collection.
3. Elle dit : « Ma décision finale est prise ! »
4. Il a l'impression que Marie ne plaisante pas.
5. Il y avait un peu de confusion avec toutes les rues et les impasses.

21A.

1. métamorphose: changement
2. analyse: étude
3. crise: problème
4. emphase: accentuation
5. hypothèse: présomption
6. dialyse: sang
7. hypnose: pendule

21B.

1. Ils ne mettent pas vraiment l'accent sur la ballade touristique parce qu'ils connaissent déjà Tours assez bien.
2. Ils vont chercher un cousin de Philippe qui étudie à Tours.
3. Il écrit sa thèse sur la crise financière du tiers-monde
4. Non, il n'a pas d'hypothèse pour sa thèse.
5. Il demande : « Est-ce que tu peux m'aider ? »

22A.

1. station: bus
2. situation: circonstance
3. réaction: réponse
4. direction: route
5. célébration: anniversaire
6. contribution: donation
7. nation: pays

22B.

1. Ils voient l'affiche pour la célébration dans la station de bus.
2. Ce sera une grande fête.
3. La célébration est intéressante pour Philippe parce qu'il veut découvrir cette belle ville et sa cuisine.
4. Sa réaction est plus sobre.
5. Il se sent plus calme.

23A.

1. université: professeur
2. difficulté: obstacle
3. impossibilité: infaisabilité
4. activité: mouvement
5. opportunité: chance
6. créativité: imagination
7. quantité: abondance

23B.

1. Elle dit que Versailles est une ville où il y a beaucoup de créativité, d'originalité et d'activité.
2. Il aime beaucoup la personnalité de cette ville.
3. Ils restent quatre jours à Versailles.
4. Non, elle croit voir une célébrité.
5. Oui, elle veut vivre à Versailles un jour. Elle dit : « Il y a beaucoup de possibilités pour nous ici. »

APPENDIX

CD TRACK LISTING

	English suffix	French suffix
Track 1 (3:57)	–al	–al
Track 2 (1:53)	–ance	–ance
Track 3 (2:36)	–ant	–ant
Track 4 (2:06)	–ar	–aire
Track 5 (2:29)	–ary	–arie
Track 6 (3:45)	–ble	–ble
Track 7 (1:57)	–ct	–ct
Track 8 (2:54)	–ence	–ence
Track 9 (2:49)	–ent	–ent
Track 10 (2:38)	–gy	–gie
Track 11 (4:01)	–ic	–ique
Track 12 (2:16)	–ical	–ique
Track 13 (1:53)	–id	–ide
Track 14 (2:53)	–ism	–isme
Track 15 (2:54)	–ist	–iste
Track 16 (3:00)	–ive	–if (–ive)
Track 17 (3:24)	–or	–eur
Track 18 (1:40)	–ory	–orie
Track 19 (2:51)	–ous	–eux (–euse)
Track 20 (2:49)	–sion	–sion
Track 21 (2:00)	–sis	–se
Track 22 (4:50)	–tion	–tion
Track 23 (2:54)	–ty	–té
Track 24 (2:54)	Pronunciation Guide	

ABOUT THE AUTHOR

Tom Means is an instructor in the Italian Department at Rutgers University, New Jersey. He owns and operates a private language school in New York City, the Means Language Center, where he conducts French, Italian, and Spanish classes for international companies and private clients.

ALSO AVAILABLE FROM HIPPOCRENE BOOKS...

INSTANT SPANISH VOCABULARY BUILDER
CD • 4,000 ENTRIES • 232 PAGES • 6 X 9 • 0-7818-0981-9 • $14.95PB • (481)

INSTANT ITALIAN VOCABULARY BUILDER
CD • 4,000 ENTRIES • 224 PAGES • 6 X 9 • 0-7818-0980-0 • $14.95PB • (476)

Instantly add thousands of words to your Spanish or Italian using word-ending patterns! Many words in Spanish and Italian are nearly the same as their English counterparts due to their common Latin origin. The only difference is the word ending. For example, you can translate most English words ending in –ance (such as "arrogance") into Spanish by changing the ending to –ancia ("arrog-*ancia*") and into Italian by changing the ending to –anza ("arrog–*anza*"). Because each of these patterns applies to hundreds of words, by learning them you can increase your vocabulary instantly.

In each book of this unique series, Tom Means describes the most common 23 or 24 word-ending patterns for the target language and provides over 4,000 words that follow them. On the accompanying CD, a native speaker demonstrates correct pronunciation of each chapter's most commonly used words and phrases.

Only language acquisition books that use word-ending patterns

■

Over 4,000 vocabulary words in each book

■

Exercises at end of each chapter

■

Perfect as classroom supplements or for self-study

■

Companion CDs teach pronunciation

FRENCH INTEREST TITLES FROM HIPPOCRENE BOOKS...

Language Guides

FRENCH-ENGLISH/ENGLISH-FRENCH DICTIONARY & PHRASEBOOK
5,500 ENTRIES • 233 PAGES • 3¾ x 7½ • 0-7818-0856-1 • $11.95PB • (128)

EMERGENCY FRENCH PHRASEBOOK
80 PAGES • 7½ x 4⅛ • 0-7818-0974-6 • $5.95PB • (455)

BEGINNER'S FRENCH
465 PAGES • 5½ x 8½ • 0-7818-0863-4 • $14.95PB • (264)

FRENCH-ENGLISH/ENGLISH-FRENCH PRACTICAL DICTIONARY
35,000 ENTRIES • 5½ x 8½ • 0-7818-0178-8 • $9.95PB • (199)

HIPPOCRENE CHILDREN'S ILLUSTRATED FRENCH DICTIONARY
English-French/French-English
- for ages 5 and up
- 500 entries with color pictures
- commonsense pronunciation for each French word
- French-English index

500 ENTRIES • 94 PAGES • 8½ x 11 • 0-7818-0847-2 • $11.95PB • (663)

FRENCH-ENGLISH DICTIONARY OF GASTRONOMIC TERMS
20,000 ENTRIES • 500 PAGES • 5½ x 8½ • 0-7818-0555-4 • $24.95PB • (655)

CAJUN FRENCH-ENGLISH/ENGLISH-CAJUN FRENCH DICTIONARY & PHRASEBOOK
At the heart of Cajun culture is a fascinating dialect of French that has survived the forces of Americanization and is still spoken by over 250,000 residents of Louisiana. With a historical overview and an introduction to the language, this book answers many common questions about Cajun French. The preface by David Cheramie, executive director of the Council for the Development of French in Louisiana (CODOFIL), offers the viewpoint of an influential leader in the movement to preserve Louisiana's unique linguistic heritage.

3,000 ENTRIES • 175 PAGES • 3¾ x 7½ • 0-7818-0915-0 • $11.95PB • (93)

History and Culture

FRANCE: AN ILLUSTRATED HISTORY
Encompassing more than 500,000 years from ancient times to the 21st century, French history is a vast body run through by manifold and, often turbulent, currents. This volume provides a succinct panorama of these cultural, political, and social currents, as well as concise analyses of their origins and effects. Complemented by 50 illustrations and maps, this text is an invaluable addition to the library of the traveler, the student, and the history enthusiast.
214 PAGES • 5 x 7 • 50 B/W PHOTOS/ILLUS./MAPS • 0-7818-0872-3 • $12.95PB • (340)

PARIS: AN ILLUSTRATED HISTORY
Paris stands as a center of culture, a leader in fashion and the arts, and a focal point in the world, where ideas meet, clash, and are redefined. In this engaging concise history, Elaine Mohktefi spans Paris' history from its modest beginnings on a bit of island in the Seine to today's thriving metropolis. Ideal for the student, traveler, or generally curious reader, this book outlines the historical context of Paris' major battles waged over religion, the monarchy, and democracy. It is complemented by over 50 illustrations.
150 PAGES • 5 x 7• 50 B/W PHOTOS/ILLUS./MAPS • 0-7818-0838-3 • $12.95PB • (136)

Literature

TREASURY OF FRENCH LOVE POEMS, QUOTATIONS & PROVERBS
In French and English
This beautiful gift volume contains poems, quotations and proverbs in French with side by side English translation. Includes elections from Baudelaire, Hugo, Rimbaud and others. Also available in audio cassette read by native French speakers and American actors.
128 PAGES • 5 x 7 • $11.95HC • 0-7818-0307-1 • (344)
CASSETTES: 0-7818-0359-4 • $12.95 • (580)

TREASURY OF FRENCH LOVE POEMS, VOLUME 2
In French and English
This anthology features love poems by classic poets and authors such as François Villon, Louise Labé, George Sand, Charles Baudelaire, Paul Éluard, and Jacques Prévert. The side-by-side English translations make these treasures of the French poetic patrimony available even to readers with little or no knowledge of French.
150 PAGES • 5 x 7 • 0-7818-0930-4 • $11.95HC • (519)

Treasury of Classic French Love Short Stories
In French and English
These 10 short stories span eight centuries of French literature. Nine celebrated French writers are represented: Marie de France, Marguerite de Navarre, Madame de Lafayette, Guy de Maupassant, Rétif de la Bretonne, Alphonse Daudet, Auguste de Villiers de l'Isle, Gabrielle-Sidonie Colette, and Jean Giono. The text includes the original French with side by side English translation.
159 PAGES • 5 X 7 • 0-7818-0511-2 • W • $11.95HC • (621)

Dictionary of 1,000 French Proverbs
Organized alphabetically by key words, this bilingual reference book is a guide to and information source for a key element of French.
131 PAGES • 5 X 8 • 0-7818-0400-0 • $11.95PB • (146)

Cuisine

Tastes of the Pyrenees, Classic and Modern
This cookbook focuses on the polyglot of cuisines of the Pyrenees region, whose mountains stretch almost 300 miles from the balmy beaches of the Mediterranean to the turbulent Atlantic coast. The recipes in this book include ones from Catalonia in both Spain and France, Roussillon, Languedoc, the Midi Pyrenees, the Basque country (*Euskal Herria*) in both France and Spain, Asturias, Navarra, and Aragón. It also includes chapters on the natural and human history that provide a background for today's cuisines of the Pyrenees. Each of the 86 recipes opens with a short narrative introduction that highlights the differences and similarities in the various cooking styles of this exciting culinary region.
296 PAGES • 6 X 9 • TWO-COLOR • 0-7818-0949-5 • $24.95HC • (405)

A Taste of Haiti
With African, French, Arabic and Amerindian influences, the food and culture of Haiti are fascinating subjects to explore. From the days of slavery to present times, traditional Haitian cuisine has relied upon staples like root vegetables, pork, fish, and flavor enhancers like *Pikliz* (picklese, or hot pepper vinegar) and *Zepis* (ground spices). This cookbook presents more than 100 traditional Haitian recipes, which are complemented by information on Haiti's history, holidays and celebrations, necessary food staples, and cooking methods. Recipe titles are presented in English, Creole, and French.
180 PAGES • 5½ X 8½ • 0-7818-0927-4 • $24.95HC • (8)

A Taste of Quebec, Second Edition

First published in 1990, A *Taste of Quebec* is the definitive guide to traditional and modern cooking in this distinctive region of Canada. Now revised and updated, this edition features over 125 new recipes and traditional favorites, along with highlights on up-and-coming new chefs, the province's best restaurants, notes of architectural and historical interest, and typical regional menus for a genuine Quebecois feast. With photos illustrating the people, the cuisine, and the land sprinkled throughout, this is *the* food lover's guide to Quebec.

200 PAGES • 8-PAGE COLOR INSERT • 7¾ X 9⅜ • 0-7818-0902-9 • $16.95PB • (32)

French Caribbean Cuisine

This marvelous cookbook contains over 150 authentic recipes from the French islands of Guadeloupe and Martinique. Favorites such as Avocado Charlotte, Pumpkin and Coconut Soup, Fish Crêpes Saintoise, and Fish Court Bouillon will beckon everyone to the table. Also included are an extensive glossary of culinary terms that will familiarize home cooks with various exotic fruits, vegetables, and fish, as well as a list of websites that specialize in Caribbean products and spices.

232 PAGES • 6 X 9 • 0-7818-0925-8 • $24.95HC • (3)

Cooking in the French Fashion
Recipes in French and English

Featuring 38 bilingual recipes, *Cooking in the French Fashion* offers unique insight into the art of contemporary French cuisine. Sample such stylish delicacies as *Blanquette de veau* (Veal Blanquette), *Artichauts vinaigrette* (Artichokes with Vinaigrette Sauce), *Gigot d'agneau aux flageolets* (Leg of Lamb with Flageolets) and *Mousse au chocolat* (Chocolate Mousse) among many others.

93 PAGES • 5 X 7 • 0-7818-0739-5 • $11.95HC • (139)